Medical Law in Japan

Medical Law in Japan

Fourth Edition

Katsunori Kai
Yuichiro Sato
Yuko Nagamizu

This book was originally published as a monograph in the International Encyclopaedia of Laws/Medical Law.

Founding Editor: Roger Blanpain
General Editor: Frank Hendrickx
Volume Editor: Herman Nys

Wolters Kluwer

Published by:
Kluwer Law International B.V.
PO Box 316
2400 AH Alphen aan den Rijn
The Netherlands
E-mail: international-sales@wolterskluwer.com
Website: www.wolterskluwer.com/en/solutions/kluwerlawinternational

Sold and distributed by:
Wolters Kluwer Legal & Regulatory U.S.
7201 McKinney Circle
Frederick, MD 21704
United States of America
E-mail: customer.service@wolterskluwer.com

ISBN 978-94-035-4112-9

e-Book: ISBN 978-94-035-4113-6
web-PDF: ISBN 978-94-035-4114-3

The Authors

Katsunori Kai, PhD, is a graduate from Kyushu University, Japan. He is a Professor at Waseda Law School, Tokyo, Japan. His major is Criminal Law (criminal negligence). He also specializes in regulation of assisted reproductive technology (ART) and withdrawal and withholding of medical care of terminal stage patients and has written books on these matters, including, *Euthanasia and Criminal Law, Death with Dignity and Criminal Law, and Protection of Human Subjects and Criminal Law*. He is an ex-director of the Japanese Association of Medical Law, the Criminal Law Society of Japan and the Councillor of Japanese Association for Bioethics, and served as a programme chair of the 25th World Association for Medical Law held at Waseda University, Japan, in August 2019.

Yuichiro Sato is a graduate from Hitotsubashi University, Japan (LLB, 1995), of Tokai University, Japan (LLM, 1997). He was an Assistant Professor at Yokohama City University School of Medicine, Japan (2000–2007), Associate Professor at Faculty of Law of Kobe Gakuin University, Japan (2007–2011), and he has been an Associate Professor at Tokyo Gakugei University, Japan since 2011. His major is Medical Law and Bioethics, especially the legal nature of parts of the human body and regulation of innovative therapy. He is a member of the governmental committee on innovative therapy and committee on pharmaceuticals, and so on. He was also a working member of the Global Ethics Observatory of United Nations Educational, Social and Cultural Organization.

The Authors

Yuko Nagamizu, LLM, is a Professor in Civil Law, Family Law, the Law of Succession and Medical Law at the Faculty of Law of Momoyama Gakuin University (St. Andrew's University) in Osaka, Japan. She graduated from Sophia University in Tokyo and received LLM from the Graduate School of Law at Sophia University, Tokyo. She has written articles on medical neglect, mature minor's right in healthcare, especially on abortion and life-sustaining medical treatment (LSMT), genetic information and family, ART and organ transplant. She was a member of the governmental committee on the amendment of ethical guidelines of medical research, and now serves as an expert panel member on the research for human specified embryos, etc. in the Ministry of Education, Culture, Sports, Science and Technology (MEXT).

Table of Contents

Table of Contents

Table of Contents

List of Abbreviations

AID	Artificial Insemination by Donor
ART	Assisted Reproductive Technology
FtM	Female to Male
GCP	Good Clinical Practice
GDP	Gross Domestic Product
GID	Gender-Identity-Disorder
GMP	Good Manufacturing Practice
HR	House of Representatives
IVF	in vitro fertilization
JAMS	Japanese Association of Medical Sciences
JMA	Japanese Medical Association
KCL	Potassium Chloride
LSMT	Life-Sustaining Medical Treatment
MEXT	Ministry of Education, Culture, Sports, Science and Technology
MHLW	Ministry of Health, Labour and Welfare
MHW	Ministry of Health and Welfare
NIPT	Non-invasive Prenatal Test
OECD	Organisation for Economic Co-operation and Development
ROP	Retinopathy of Prematurity
SMON	Subacute Myelo-Optico-Neuropathy
US	United States
WMA	World Medical Association

List of Abbreviations

Japanese Titles

Act on Nurses and Midwives 保健師助産師看護師法
Anatomical Gift Act 医学及び歯学の教育のための献体に関する法律
Anatomy and Hold of Cadaver Act 死体解剖保存法
Child Welfare Act 児童福祉法
Doctors Act 医師法
Eugenics Protection Act 優生保護法
Health Insurance Act 健康保険法
Japanese Association of Medical Law 日本医事法学会
Kan-pou 漢方
Maternity Protection Act 母体保護法
Medical Care Act 医療法
Ministry of Education, Culture, Sports, Science and Technology 文部科学省
Ministry of Finance 財務省
Ministry of Health, Labour and Welfare 厚生労働省
Ministry of Health and Welfare 厚生省
National Health Insurance Act 国民健康保険法
Pharmaceutical Affairs Act 医薬品、医療機器等の品質、有効性及び安全性の確保等に関する法律
Pharmacists Act 薬剤師法
Regional Public Health Act 地域保健法

General Introduction

Chapter 1. General Background of the Country

§1. Geography and Climate

1. Japan is an Asian country that is isolated from the Eurasian continent by the Sea of Japan. It consists of many islands in the Pacific Ocean; the relatively large islands are Hokkaido, Honshu (the main island), Shikoku and Kyushu, from north to south, and the Ryukyu Islands south of Kyushu.

Some 126 million people live in 378,000 square kilometres, but as the land is mountainous, a disproportionate number of people live in flatlands near coastal areas. In the 1960s, younger generations moved from rural areas to large cities, which led to depopulation and ageing in rural areas, where people have relatively poor healthcare (*see* Part III Chapter 2).

The climate is predominantly temperate but varies greatly from north to south. Hokkaido belongs to the subarctic zone whereas some Ryukyu Islands are tropical. In the north and west, there is much snow in winter, but not in the Pacific coastal belt zone, where large cities such as Tokyo and Osaka are situated.

§2. Political and Judicial System

2. Japan is a democratic country. The Japanese Constitution defines the emperor (Ten-nou) as a symbol of national unity. Legislative, executive and judicial powers are separate from each other.

The Diet is the only legislative organ (Article 41 of the Japanese Constitution). It has two houses, the House of Representatives (HR) and the House of Councillors (HC). The HR term is four years, and the HC term is six years. A prime minister is elected from among the members of the HR.

Executive power is delegated to the cabinet. The Ministry of Health, Labour and Welfare (MHLW) is the branch responsible for health and medical care. Originally, the MHLW was established as the Ministry of Health, when it became independent from the then Ministry of Interior Affairs (and National Police) just before WWII. It aimed to make the nation ‘healthier’ to raise more healthy soldiers.

The Ministry of Education, Culture, Sports, Science and Technology (MEXT) also has authority over some medical matters. The MEXT governs universities (and university hospitals) and research activities such as therapeutic cloning and research using Human Embryonic Stem (hES) cells.[1]

Local governments (especially prefectures) are responsible for healthcare administration under the national policy and advice of the MHLW. A governor of a prefecture was deemed as an officer of the central government before WWII. And until recently (1999) not a prefecture but a governor was delegated from the central government in some areas, including healthcare, which meant local assemblies could not make ordinances controlling the delegated affairs. This delegation system was abolished, but, partly because of the highly specialized nature of healthcare administration, the MHLW makes relatively rigid national policy and local governments do not have discretion.

3. Japan is a civil law country, so the accumulation of court judgments does not constitute law in a strict sense. Japanese courts do not issue declaratory judgments, so the role of judgment is limited to restitution of damage after accidents, except for temporary injunctions. Some few malpractice cases are tried in criminal courts.

§3. Population and Vital Statistics

4. Japan's total population was 126,417,000 on 1 September 2018. The number of males was 61,515,000, and the number of females was 64,901,000. Japan has a very strict immigration policy, so most inhabitants are Japanese (124,259,000). The number of foreigners who do not register may not be correctly reflected.

Distribution by age is as follows:

- 12.2% under 15 years old;
- 59.7% 15–65 years old; and
- 28.1% over 65 years old (and 14.2% are over 75).

Life expectancy at birth was 81.25 years for males and 87.32 years for females, as of 2018, which are said to be third and second in the world.

Japan's birth rate was decreasing: in 2017, the total fertility rate was 1.43. The perinatal mortality rate was 3.5 per 1,000, and the neonatal mortality rate was 0.9 per 1,000 in 2017, about which a government report says they vary twofold among prefectures.

The main causes of death in 2017 were neoplasm (rate in all death; males – 3.19%, females – 23.5%), cardiovascular disease (males – 13.9%, females – 16.7%) and cerebrovascular disease (males – 7.7%, females – 8.7%).

1. Described below in Part II Ch. 3 §7.

Chapter 2. General Description of the Healthcare System

§1. General Overview of the Healthcare System

I. Brief History

5. Japan became open to foreign countries in the mid-nineteenth century. Until then, doctors practised traditional Chinese medicine (Kan-pou). There was no systematic education and licensing system for Kan-pou doctors. Their main work was prescribing and providing medicine at the doctor's house, and their fee was called a 'drug fee'. This tradition had three effects on the contemporary healthcare system in Japan:

(1) Japan did not have separate clinics and hospitals;[2]
(2) any doctor could establish a hospital freely; and
(3) Japan did not have prescription pharmacies (pharmacies sold mainly non-prescription drugs).

These tendencies have been changing in the past twenty years.

6. After opening to foreign countries, the government had to cope with controlling contagious diseases such as cholera and decided to adopt Western medicine (mainly that of Germany) and established national medical schools and examinations for 'doctors' (not traditional Kan-pou doctors). However, the Japanese government did not spend money (and prohibited local government from spending money) to establish public hospitals. Therefore, many hospitals were established as private clinics and later became hospitals. During the depression following WWI, however, hospitals/clinics in rural areas had financial difficulties, and doctors closed them. Tuberculosis spread uncontrolled, and the Department of the Army demanded the establishment of a public health system. Ultimately, a fundamental healthcare system, including national health insurance and regional public health offices, was established just before and during WWII.

7. After WWII, the political system was drastically changed, and the Constitution of Japan was established in 1947. It provides that all people shall have the right to maintain the minimum standards of wholesome and cultured living and that the State shall use its endeavours for the promotion and extension of social welfare and security, and of public health. But the fundamental system of social security and public health remained the same as the above pre-war system.

---

2. The Medical Care Act defines a hospital as an institution which has twenty beds or more, whereas a clinic has fewer than twenty beds (Arts 1–5).

II. Overview

8. Healthcare is provided mainly by private hospitals/clinics. The breakdown is as follows in Table 1.

Table 1 Types of Hospitals and Number of Beds

	Hospitals			*Medical Clinics*		*Dental Clinics*
	Number	*Total Number of Beds*	*Average Number of Beds*	*Number*	*Total Number of Beds*	*Number*
TOTAL	8,216	1,504,903	183	103,637	84,971	68,093
NATIONAL						
MHLW	14	4,239	303	20	–	–
Independent Administrative Institution	140	52,773	377	–	–	–
National University	47	32,621	694	148	–	–
Workers' Compensation	32	12,142	379	–	–	–
National Centre	8	4,110	514	–	–	–
Regional Medical Center	57	15,242	267	5	–	–
Others	23	3,515	153	365	2,167	3
PUBLIC						
Prefecture	194	50,963	263	276	186	7
City and Village	604	122,149	202	3,071	2,052	253

	Hospitals			*Medical Clinics*		*Dental Clinics*
	Number	*Total Number of Beds*	*Average Number of Beds*	*Number*	*Total Number of Beds*	*Number*
Local Independent Institution	114	44,484	390	34	17	–
Red Cross	91	34,704	381	204	19	–
Other Public	190	55,885	294	118	54	1
Insurers of Social Health Insurance	48	15,021	313	436	0	6
PRIVATE						
Corporation in Civil Code	203	50,283	248	505	192	99
Corporation in Medical Law	5,685	840,579	148	44,871	65,618	15,536
Private University	114	55,957	491	191	38	20
Corporation of Social Welfare	198	33,612	170	10,227	358	38
CO-OP	82	13,679	167	297	224	49
For Profit Company	29	8,054	278	1,604	10	13
Other Company	202	42,296	209	882	330	125

	Hospitals			*Medical Clinics*		*Dental Clinics*
	Number	*Total Number of Beds*	*Average Number of Beds*	*Number*	*Total Number of Beds*	*Number*
Personal Doctor	141	12,595	89	40,383	13,706	51,943

Source: MHLW, 31 May 2021.

9. The number of medical doctors was 319,480 on 31 December 2016, which means 250 per 100,000 people. The average term of hospitalization is around 15.6 days in a general unit and 256.7 days in a psychological unit.[3] These terms have been shortened but remain longer than those of other developed counties. It should be noted that acute and long-term care units are not strictly distinguished in the Medical Care Act, and the term for 'general unit' includes both.[4]

§2. REGULATION OF THE HEALTHCARE SYSTEM

10. Hospitals and clinics are governed by the Medical Care Act (1948). Originally, there was a free establishment policy for hospitals, which meant that the government did not have control over the private establishment of hospitals. But the Medical Care Act was revised in 1985 and now provides that the governors of each prefecture should make programmes for healthcare in which the number of needed beds should be fixed according to the formula provided by the MHLW. If the actual number exceeds the 'needed' number in an area, it is factually impossible to establish another hospital or increase the number of beds. The governor shall give 'advice' not to establish another hospital or not to increase the number of beds, and if hospitals go against this advice, such hospitals would not be appointed as providers of socialized health insurance.

11. The Act sets out many duties. Administrators of hospitals and clinics must supervise doctors, dentists, pharmacists and other employees (Article 15), and hospital administrators must provide a doctor/doctors on night duty (Article 16). While this latter duty does not apply to clinic administrators, they must ensure that prompt treatment within the clinic, as well as consultation with other hospitals and clinics, shall be available (Article 13). Hospitals must have enough doctors, nurses and other medical technicians to comply with regulations (Article 21 and Regulation 19) and must have facilities such as consulting rooms and operating rooms (Article 21).

If a governor of a prefecture thinks that a hospital or clinic lacks the manpower or has hygienic deficiencies, he/she may issue an administrative order to increase the number of employees, rebuild or restrict its operation (Articles 23-2 and 24). The governor has the authority to inspect hospitals and clinics when he/she thinks it necessary (Article 25), and hospitals are regularly inspected once a year. These inspections have not always been successful in detecting problematic conditions; sometimes, abusive treatment of patients has been discovered by whistle blowing, not by the inspection.

---

3. It is indicated that they do not reflect the actual hospitalization term. Takumi Nishi et al., *Study of the Indicators of Affordable Healthcare Planning Using Electronic Medical Claim Data*, 7 Iryou Fukushi Keiei Marketing Kenkyuu 1 (2012), available at http://www.hc-market.net/paper/hcm2012 10.pdf.
4. At one time, 'nursing care unit' (Ryouyou-Byoushou, in which patients with need of relatively low-level medical care) was included in 'general unit'. Now, it is an independent unit but still situated in a hospital. In Japan, a nursing home is not considered to be a medical facility, so nursing care to elder people is still provided in hospitals. The average term of stay in such units was 312.4 days in 2018.

§3. Financing of Healthcare

12. In the fiscal year 2017, national medical costs exceeded the Japanese Yen (JPY) 40 trillion (42.138 trillion), which is JPY 332,000 per capita. This does not include the costs for a normal delivery nor payment for a private room in a hospital (a four-bedroom is standard in Japanese health insurance, and to be admitted to a one- or two-bedroom one must make an additional payment which is not covered by the national health insurance, except when admission to the room is indicated for medical reasons). Nationally, medical costs comprise 11.2% of the Gross Domestic Product in 2015, which is the third of thirty countries of the Organisation for Economic Co-operation and Development.

Almost all Japanese healthcare is covered under socialized health insurance, and some costs are borne under the national budget. In the 2017 national budget, JPY 11.4 trillion was spent on medical insurance from a total budget of some 100 trillion. The Ministry of Finance and the MHLW cooperate in establishing the 'price' of each medical procedure under the socialized health insurance plan (also described below).

§4. Health Insurance

13. Japan has a national health insurance system, which means all people of Japanese nationality are covered under one of several plans. Foreigners who live in Japan legally – that is, who register with local governments as foreigners – and who will be in Japan for more than one year may be covered under the national health insurance scheme.

14. Original company-based health insurance was established by the Health Insurance Act (which was enacted in 1922 and began providing insurance programmes in 1927)[5] as a mixture of health insurance and workers' compensation. The government contracted with the Japanese Medical Association (JMA) for the provision of medical care, and JMA determined the amount of reimbursement. This was revised during WWII with the aim of centralizing power within the government, including the appointment of hospitals on behalf of many insurers and the pricing of medical care. This wartime scheme has been maintained generally until recently.

Today, large companies have their own health insurers, whereas employees of smaller companies are covered by the governmental insurer.[6] Family members of those workers are also covered. Employers and employees both pay the premiums (almost 1:1).

---

5. Originally planned for 1923. The delay was due to a big earthquake in the Kanto area which caused disaster in Tokyo.
6. The Social Insurance Agency (Shakai-hoken-chou, an agency under the MHLW) and Local Offices for Social Insurance (Chihou-shakai-hoken-jimu-kyoku) did clerical work for health insurance for almost eighty-five years, but the Social Insurance Agency has been widely accused of inefficient and unclear work. From October 2008, Kyokai Kenpo has been responsible for clerical work regarding health insurance; the premium varies among prefectures depending on the total amount of medical

15. People not covered by the Health Insurance Act are covered by the National Health Insurance Act, and this means that Japan has had a 'national health insurance system' since the enforcement of the latter Act in 1961. Some self-employed people (doctors and lawyers) establish their own insurers, but most people under the Act are covered by the insurers of local governments. Compared with the Health Insurance Act, where the employee's burden is half of the total cost, people covered only under the National Health Insurance Act pay much higher premiums, resulting in restricted access for relatively poor and elderly people. Furthermore, the premium is calculated per family, so if a family fails to pay the premium, all members of the family have to pay 100% of doctor/hospital fees at the time of service (70% of which may be reimbursed later). This means that children in relatively poor families may not receive healthcare because their parents cannot pay the premium. It is reported that the government will cover children younger than 16 (until they graduate junior high school) even if their parents fail to pay the premium.

16. In both these systems, hospitals and clinics are appointed as providers of socialized health insurance by the government, and prices of each medical procedure[7] are also fixed by the government. The patient's co-payment is 30%; later reimbursement is provided for costs in excess of about USD 600 per month. The table of prices is amended every two years.

---

costs within the prefecture. This means that people in rural prefectures (many of them elderly) pay higher premiums than residents of urban prefectures.

7. Hospitals and clinics are reimbursed by fee-for-service. But the MHLW wants hospital payments to be fixed by diagnosis, like DRG-PPS in the United States. Most large and acute-care hospitals (1,391 hospitals out of about total number of hospitals 8,500, and one-half of all beds) are now being reimbursed by DPC (Diagnosis Procedure Combination). The prices for prescription drugs are also fixed by the government. In 2016 the price for OPDIVO (nivolumab) was cut in half.

Chapter 3. Medical Law

§1. Definitions and Functions of Medical Law

17. As in many other countries, medical law in Japan is a relatively new academic area. It cuts across traditional legal fields such as constitutional law, civil law and criminal law. Of course, each traditional field has a relationship with medicine, for example, malpractice in tort law and informed consent in criminal law, but recognition of medical law as an independent field occurred in the 1960s. The Japanese Association of Medical Law was established in 1969; half of its members are from the medical field, and the other half are (mainly academic) lawyers.

In the civil law field, malpractice and Yakugai (unexpected adverse drug reaction) litigation have produced new theories and contributed to the body of medical law. In the penal law field, not so many cases have been raised to the criminal court level, but recently many doctors have accused police and the office of prosecutors of trying to press charges; this has a negative effect on medical practice.

§2. Sources of Medical Law

I. International Law and Codes

18. The Japanese government signs many treaties and conventions, but it is not clear whether these treaties have any legal effect without the enactment of corresponding statutes (usually treaties are not self-executing). Of course, such treaties and conventions do have symbolic meaning. For example, the International Covenant on Civil and Political Rights and Declaration of Helsinki (World Medical Association (WMA)) were referred to in a plaintiff's claim in one clinical trial case.[8] The Declaration of Helsinki is also referred to in governmental guidelines on medical research,[9] although the declaration was issued by WMA, which is not a governmental organization, so it seems to have no binding power.

II. National Sources

19. The Constitution of Japan (1946) provides that all people shall have the right to live a healthy life and that the State must improve social welfare, social security and public health. This provision is the supreme source in medical law. Delegated statutes are as follows:

– Doctors Act (which provides for the licensing and duties of medical doctors);

---

8. 1733 Hanreijihou 70 (Nagoya Dist. Ct., 24 Mar. 2000).
9. Ethical Guidelines for Medical and Health Research Involving Human Subjects, issued by the MHLW and MEXT. An English translation is available at http://www.mhlw.go.jp/file/06-Seisakujouhou-10600000-Daijinkanboukouseikagakuka/0000080278.pdf. We will address this later, in Part II Ch. 3, §7.

- Act on Nurses and Midwives and other acts providing for the licensing and duties of co-medicals;
- Medical Care Act (which provides for the regulation of hospitals and clinics);
- Regional Public Health Act (which establishes public health offices); and
- Health Insurance Act, the National Health Insurance Act and other health insurance statutes;
- General statutes such as the Civil Code and Penal Code are also applied to medical matters in litigation.

20. Japan is not a common law country, but decisions of courts are also important, because the terms of those statutes are broad, and they must be construed by courts in individual cases.

Part I. The Medical Profession

Chapter 1. Access to the Medical Profession

§1. Medical Education

I. Undergraduate Medical Education

21. There were 80 medical schools in Japan, with a total capacity of 7,625 for the fiscal year 2007; until FY 2020 it has been increased to 9,320. All medical schools are under the authority of, and supervised by, the MEXT. Students must pass a national examination run by MHLW to become doctors. The JMA is a voluntary organization of medical doctors (described below), and it has no say in the medical school curriculum or in the national exam.

The term of study in medical schools is six years, whereas, in other undergraduate schools such as law, economics and physics, it is four years. Entrance exams for medical schools are, generally, very difficult because of the competition among 'good' high school students. Tuition in private medical schools costs very high (between JPY 5 million and JPY 10 million per year).

As doctor shortage became a social problem, as described below, the MEXT decided to increase the capacity of medical schools, but the shortage is likely to continue for some time due to a time-lag in increasing the number of medical doctors.

II. Medical Education after Graduation

22. After WWII, Japan instituted an 'intern system' modelled on the United States (US), which includes one year of training after graduation and before taking the national exam. This system was highly criticized because the interns were used as 'raw recruits' in 'Ikyoku' without systematic education at university hospitals. After campus strife in many universities, the system was abolished in 1968, and a voluntary post-graduate education system was introduced.

This two-year education *after* the national exam meant that all trainees had doctors' licenses, and a medical graduate who did not get this education and training was able to be registered as a medical doctor and was able to practice if he/she has passed the national exam. So, the Doctors Act was amended in 2004 to make this training compulsory. A medical doctor who does not get this post-graduate training may not become a hospital/clinic administrator.

Until 2004, some university hospitals paid less than JPY 100,000 per month as a scholarship to the trainee, and trainees had to do extra work at other hospitals, mainly on the night shift. After the 2004 amendment, hospitals had to start paying an adequate salary to the trainees. In addition, the court decided that the trainee is a 'worker' with regard to workers' compensation and minimum wage laws,[10] and universities and hospitals have the responsibility of making sure trainees do not suffer Karoushi (death from overwork).[11] In Japan, working time is limited to forty hours per week (but extra work is common, especially for physicians), and the MHLW (which also controls labour regulations) has mandated that hospitals should apply this limitation to trainees.[12]

Until recently, many young doctors took their post-graduate training at their own university hospitals, but now a lot of private hospitals are allowed to provide this training. Some doctors prefer to train in well-known private hospitals, resulting in a serious doctor shortage in university hospitals in rural areas (*see also* Part III Chapter 2).[13]

III. Graduate Medical Education

23. Medical doctors often pursue graduate education after completing medical school. The term for this graduate education is four years. Graduate school students (who passed the national exam and are medical doctors) often have to see patients as part of their training, but they are not paid. So it follows that in the two-year period described above, new doctors are paid, but after these two years, if they enter graduate school, they are not paid for patient care.

§2. Licensing of Medical Doctors and Specialities

24. As described above, one must pass a national exam to obtain a medical license. The MHLW grants licences and initiates disciplinary sanctions.

To take the national exam, one must:

(1) graduate from a medical school;
(2) pass a preliminary exam and have one year of experience in medical practice; or

---

10. Not reported (Osaka Dist. Ct., Sakai Branch, 29 Aug. 2001).
11. 879 Roudouhanrei 22 (Osaka App. Ct., 15 Jul. 2004).
12. Cf., in the US, interns' working time is limited to eighty hours per week. George J. Annas, *The Rights of Patients* 71 (New York University Press 2004).
13. Once the trainees got two-year training in major specialities such as internal medicine, surgery, emergency, paediatrics, and obstetrics and gynaecology. In 2009, MHLW issued guidelines which permit each hospital to shorten the 'general' training (six months for internal medicine, three month for emergency medicine and one month for regional healthcare), which meant hospitals (especially university hospitals) might provide training of speciality for the rest time. This guidelines also provide restriction of the number of trainees, of which the purpose was that more trainees would stay in university hospitals.

(3) graduate from a foreign medical school or have a foreign medical licence approved by the MHLW (Doctors Act Article 11).

Conditions (2) and (3) are quite rare;[14] in usual practice, one must graduate from a Japanese medical school.[15]

25. A medical doctor may practice every speciality, regardless of his/her experience. This has long been the subject of criticism, but Taro Takemi,[16] a famous chairman of the JMA, strongly opposed restriction of speciality, citing an example that an internist treating diabetes patients also treats their eye problems.

Recently, however, many medical colleges and associations have begun giving exams for specialities (such as internal medicine), and doctors have to attend annual meetings and additional conferences to keep up their specialist status. But this has little effect in practice and has no binding power; any doctor may practice all kinds of medicine and advertise 'internal medicine', 'surgery', etc. regardless of his/her speciality.[17] Of course, doctors often hesitate to see patients outside their area of speciality, because of the fear of malpractice suit.

§3. Manpower Planning: Freedom of Establishment

26. The Japanese government had a policy of free establishment of hospitals and issued relatively many licences to private universities to run medical schools in the 1970s to increase the number of doctors. But in the mid-1980s, the Ministry of Finance and the Ministry of Health and Welfare (MHW) used the 'supplier induced demand hypothesis' to restrict the number of doctors and hospital beds. As described above, in 1981, the total capacity of medical schools was 8,280, but it decreased to 7,625 in 2007. As the doctor shortage became acute, however, the government decided to increase the number. The capacity in 2014 was 9,061, as described above.

27. The Medical Care Act was revised in 1985 and demanded each prefecture to make a plan, the main purpose of which was to calculate the 'needed' number of hospital beds. If the actual number of beds exceeds the calculated one, the governor (the approval of the governor is needed for the establishment of hospitals and clinics with beds and increasing the number of beds) advises the applicants not to open

14. 1757 Hanreijihou 51 (Tokyo App. Ct., 14 Jun. 2001) was a case on the refusal of a graduate of a Chinese medical university to take national exam. The court revoked the refusal by MHLW because MHLW had not provided enough reason required by the Administrative Procedure Act.
15. Recently, Iwate Medical School invited two Chinese doctors (an obstetrician/gynaecologist and a paediatrician), but they are 'practicing' doctors in medical school without the above approval, so they are not approved to take the national exam.
16. It is interesting that he strongly opposed the 'general practitioner' system, because he saw GPs in national medical care (such as National Health Service in England) as deprived of a speciality by the government.
17. But to advertise 'anaesthesia', hospitals and clinics must have anaesthesia specialist(s) who is/are permitted by the MHLW. In addition to this system, new specialist system had been supposed to become effective in 2017, but it was suspended for one year and started in 2018. https://jmsb.or.jp/.

the proposed hospital in the area (Article 30-7), and it will not be appointed as a provider of health insurance if the hospital was established against that advice, so in practice this calculation of number of beds hinders newcomers. The amendment in 2014 provides another system; all hospitals must report the function of their wards (Intensive Acute, Acute, Convalescent, and Chronic), and if the function exceeds the need of the regional hospitals should attend to a 'committee for consultation' for reducing the function (Articles 30-13 to 30-18).

§4. Responsibility of the Central and Local Governments

28. As described above, Article 25 of the Japanese Constitution provides the duty of promotion of social welfare, social security and public health. But the Japanese government has not provided medical care on its own. During WWII, the government established Nihon Iryou Dan (Japanese medical organization) and let it run national hospitals. The Iryou Dan was abolished after the war, and some hospitals were privatized. Since then, national and municipal hospitals have been privatized as well, and, as stated above, medical care is mainly provided by private hospitals. Recently, hospitals run by the local governments have been experiencing staff shortages and deficits, and some of them have closed.

Chapter 2. Practice of Medicine

§1. LEGAL CONDITIONS FOR THE PRACTICE OF MEDICINE

29. The Doctors Act makes medical practice exclusive to doctors. Although there is no doubt that nurses and other co-medical practitioners may practise under a doctor's direction (*see* Part III), there is a concern that doctors may hire an unlicensed worker to help in medical procedures. The Tokyo Appellate Court decided that:

> considering that the law makes the practice of medicine exclusive to someone with a license, the area where doctors may use someone without a license as a helper should be narrowly construed; he/she should be so-called doctor's hands, that is, when the doctor can watch what they do, there is no risk of harm to patients, and he/she does only mechanical work with little discretion.[18]

It is generally held that medical procedures shall be lawful with:

(1) informed consent;
(2) *lege artis*; and
(3) subjective purpose of treatment.

Bodily invasion without any one of these three may be unlawful in civil law, and if harm occurs, it could be considered assault and battery in criminal law (there are no reported cases of intentional crime; doctors would be prosecuted as having been negligent[19]). The need for informed consent is provided in the Medical Care Act (Article 1-4).

30. So-called marginal medical procedures (Igyou-Ruiji-Koui) such as Judo therapy, traditional massage and acupuncture are regulated by statutes and only allowed with a licence. Chiropractic is not regulated, so it may be done by someone who does not have any licence. Other types of complementary and alternative medicine are not regulated; 'Homeopathy' became a problem in 2010 after a newborn died to whom a midwife did not provide Vitamin K.

18. 691 Hanreitaimuzu 152 (Tokyo App. Ct., 23 Feb. 1989).
19. In *Fujimi Sanfujinka* (an obstetrics and gynaecology case), it was claimed that the owner of a hospital (not a medical doctor) directed doctors to remove patients' healthy uteri with patients' consent based on fraudulent information that uteri were 'a mess' (so patients' consent seemed to be invalid). In civil litigation, the court said as obiter dicta that defendants' act would correspond to be assault and battery in criminal cases, but the prosecutor did not bring this case to court on the charge of assault and battery, so whether the removal was a criminal offence or not was not decided. In this case, only breach of prohibition of medical practice without licence was charged (Tokyo App. Ct., 23 Feb. 1989, described in *supra* n. 1).

§2. Illegal Practice of Medicine

31. As mentioned above, a doctor's title and practice are exclusive; the Doctors Act prohibits 'the use of title of doctor' (Article 18) and 'providing medical procedure as a practice' (Article 17). The latter has some room for discussion because the meanings of both 'medical procedure' ('Ikoui' in Japanese) and 'practice' ('Gyou') are open. Courts and the MHLW say that 'medical procedure' is an act which may bring harm to patients if it is done without the knowledge and skill of doctors, and that 'practice' means the intent to repetitious and continuous action. It is said that self-care and care within the family would be excluded from this prohibition. Home care, such as self-injection or injection by family members of insulin in diabetics and clotting factor in haemophiliacs (this caused Human Immunodeficiency Virus infection in the late 1970s and 1980s), suction of phlegm in the care of disabled and Amyotrophic Lateral Sclerosis patients at home, and home oxygen therapy, is widespread in Japan. Although it is not clear whether these procedures may be done in schools by teachers, a committee under the MHLW, in a report in 2004, permitted teachers to perform suction of phlegm in schools for physically handicapped and mentally retarded children. The use of an Automated External Defibrillator by anyone in an emergency situation is also permitted by the MHLW.

The Doctors Act provides that offenders of the above prohibition shall be sentenced to imprisonment of three years or less, a penalty of JPY 1 million or less, or both. There is similar prohibition in acts on nurses and midwives, physical and occupational therapists, and others. As a general rule, the Supreme Court held that prohibition of therapy which has some risk of harm to human health[20] is reasonable and constitutional (14 Keishu 33 (Sup. Ct., 27 January 1960)); Article 22 of the Japanese Constitution guarantees the freedom of choice of his/her occupation, but this may be limited based on public welfare. In actual cases, a defendant who performed vision screening and fitting of contact lenses was found guilty (sentenced to eight months' (an employer physician) and five months' (an employee) imprisonment with suspension (appeal dismissed, 51 Keishu 671 (Sup. Ct., 30 September 1997))); intubation by a dentist without the actual supervision of medical doctor during training was a violation of the prohibition and the director of the emergency department of the hospital was sentenced to a fine of JPY 60,000 (not reported (Sapporo Dist. Ct., 28 March 2003, approved by Sapporo App. Ct., 6 March 2008)). A doctor who let persons without any licence suture a fascia and did ultrasound and electrocardiogram (ECG) was determined to be an offender under the Act on Nurses and Midwives and was sentenced to eight months' imprisonment with suspension (appeal dismissed, 691 Hanreitaimuzu 152 (Tokyo App. Ct., 23 February 1989)). Furthermore whether 'irezumi' (traditional Japanese tattoo) is also a medical procedure which needs a doctor's licence or not has been a hot topic of debate; a judgment (1370 Hanreitaimuzu 159 (Tokyo Dist. Ct., 9 March 1990)) distinguished 'art

20. Dissenting opinion said that even if the procedure itself has no physical risk, there might be some risk that people rely on such a medical procedure and miss the chance to receive 'normal' medical treatment, so the prohibition would be constitutional regardless of the physical harm in the procedure.

make' from 'irezumi' saying the latter was accepted socially, and an appellate court in another case judged not guilty in 'irezumi' case (Osaka App. Ct., 14 November 2018) noted that the prohibited acts should be understood as acts with the intent of practising medicine, and the supreme court approved this decision (74 Keishu 581 (Sup. Ct. 16 September 2020)).

Chapter 3. Control over the Practice of Medicine

§1. Licence and Disciplinary Action by the MHLW

32. As described above, the MHLW has the authority to give licenses and take disciplinary action. Doctors Act provides that if a doctor has:

(1) a mental or physical disability which may cause incompetence;
(2) addiction to narcotics, cannabis or opium;
(3) a conviction resulting in a fine and/or imprisonment;
(4) been convicted of another crime or misconduct concerning medicine; or
(5) been guilty of a degrading action, the Minister may take one or more of the following administrative measures:
   (a) warning;
   (b) suspension of license for not more than three years; or
   (c) revocation of license (Article 7(2)).

The Minister has to consult with the Committee of Medical Affairs (of which the President of the JMA is a member) and hold an administrative hearing for the suspected doctor. Disciplinary actions are modest in number.[21] For five years from 1 April 2000 to 31 March 2005, the total number was two-hundred and ten (including nineteen revocations): sixteen for breach of the Doctors Act or other co-medical act; fifteen (including one revocation) for illegal use/handling of narcotics, cannabis and stimulant drugs; three (including one revocation) for murder and assault and battery; eight for traffic accidents, twenty-six for medical malpractice; twenty-eight (including seven revocations) for obscene action; fifteen for taking bribes; twenty-two (including one revocation) for larceny and fraud in criminal cases; three for forgery of documents; thirteen (including one revocation) for tax evasion; thirty-two for fraud in claiming reimbursement of health insurance; and twenty-nine (including eight revocations) for other reasons. The MHLW has no independent source for criminal cases, so it lets the Ministry of Justice report the prosecution of doctors. In almost all cases of unacceptable conduct (not only (3) but also (4) and (5) above), disciplinary actions are taken after the criminal convictions,[22] except in monetary fraud in health insurance cases, about which the MHLW may get a direct

21. It has been pointed that the negativity of disciplinary action (and/or lack of self-regulation) leads to a greater role for criminal law. *See* Robert B. Leflar, *Law and Patient Safety in the United States and Japan*, in *Readings in Comparative Health Law & Bioethics* 124, 126 (Timothy Stoltzfus Jost ed., 2nd ed., Carolina Academic Press 2007).
22. In cases following criminal conviction, the judgment of the criminal court can be used in the disciplinary proceeding. So the disciplinary proceeding need not have included a fact-finding process, other than the hearing of the subject (it is subject to the Administrative Procedure Act because the action is taken by the Minister). The actions are seldom contested; in fact, there are a few reported cases on disciplinary action (35 Shoumugeppou 512 (Sup. Ct., 1 Jul. 1988) and 1950 Hanreijihou 49 (Tokyo Dist. Ct., 24 Feb. 2006)), where the plaintiff did not argue about the fact itself; on the other hand, court rejected request for temporary injunction by a doctor with (some extent of) fact-finding (Tokyo Dist. Ct., 26 Apr. 2005 (not reported)).

report from a local department. In some serious cases, the MHLW will take disciplinary action before the criminal procedure.

Until recently, the doctor who had become the subject of disciplinary action only needed to wait out the term. This was strongly criticized, and compulsory re-education became a hot issue, resulting in an MHLW report in 2005.[23] Now the subjects must attend one day (in case of warning) or two days of lectures (in more serious actions), and take on additional work (e.g., those who become the subjects of one-year suspensions or more must take training).[24]

§2. The Role of JMA and Associations/Colleges

33. Before WWII, medical doctors had to be members of the JMA, but according to the direction of the General Headquarter, JMA became a voluntary association of doctors. About 60% of Japanese doctors are members of JMA, and most members practice at their own clinics. Thus, where the interests of practising doctors and large hospitals conflict, it is generally felt that JMA tends to favour the former.

JMA has issued sets of guidelines, for example, professional guidelines for doctors (Ishi-no-Shokugyo-Rinri-Shishin),[25] guidelines on the provision of medical information, and guidelines concerning terminal care.

34. Medical associations/colleges also issue guidelines. For example, the Japan Society of Obstetrics and Gynaecology issues guidelines and statements on Assisted Reproductive Technology (ART), research use of embryos and gametes, and sex selection. The Japan Society for Transplantation issues guidelines which provide the requirements on living donation.[26] But doctors who are not members of the society are free from these guidelines, so the Society of Obstetrics and Gynaecology asked the government to enact a statute on ART, and discussions took place at a committee under the Science Council of Japan (*see* Part II Chapter 3 §3 D).[27] Furthermore, investigations into the actual state of some special medical procedures are carried out by associations. For example, the Japan Society of Obstetrics and Gynaecology handles registration of in vitro fertilization and embryo transfer (IVF-ET),[28] and the Japan Society for Transplantation gathers information on recipients and living donors, following the Declaration of Istanbul[29] and guiding principles of the World Health Organization.[30]

---

23. www.mhlw.go.jp/shingi/2005/04/s0422-8.html.
24. www.mhlw.go.jp/shingi/2007/06/dl/s0606-4h.pdf.
25. www.med.or.jp/nichikara/syokurin.html.
26. The Organ Transplantation Act regulates only deceased donation, except for the prohibition of sales of organs. So living donation is not regulated by OTA and this set of guidelines is the only requirement on living donation; according to a MHLW circular, hospitals must comply with this requirement to get reimbursement from health insurance.
27. A report was issued in April 2008: www.scj.go.jp/ja/info/kohyo/pdf/kohyo-20-t56-1.pdf.
28. www.jsog.or.jp/activity/report.html.
29. Lancet. 5 Jul. 2008; 372(9632): 5–6.
30. http://apps.who.int/gb/ebwha/pdf_files/WHA63/A63_R22-en.pdf.

§3. Professional Liability

I. Introduction

35. There is no special statute on professional liability, so general provisions of the Civil Code and Penal Code are applied to doctors' malpractice; civil liability is either breach of contract (Articles 415 and 416) or torts (Articles 709–724), and criminal liability will be judged on accidental infliction of injury in practice (Article 211) as in a traffic accident.[31]

II. Civil Liability

A. *Torts*

36. Article 709 of the Japanese Civil Code provides that those who infringe rights or legally protected interests of others intentionally or negligently shall be liable to compensate the damage resulted. The requirements are:

(1) intention or negligence;[32]
(2) infringement of rights or interests;
(3) damage; and
(4) causation.

The plaintiff has the burden of proof for all of these. Article 715 provides that those who employ such a person shall be liable as respondeat superior unless the employer proves either that he/she has exercised reasonable care in supervising the wrongdoer or that the result is unavoidable.

Negligence is based on foreseeability and/or avoidability. If a person does not foresee (and does not avoid) the bad result, and a reasonable person might foresee and avoid it in such a situation, he/she shall be found as negligent. Thus, foreseeability and avoidability of a reasonable doctor make the standard of care in malpractice litigation. But it is hard for the plaintiff, who is a layperson, to prove negligence.

Extinctive prescription is three years in general, and five years in cases of harm to human life and body, after the victim knows the damage and the perpetrator or twenty years after the accident (Article 724, 724-2).

The plaintiff would be the patient concerned or successors when the patient dies. The defendant would be the doctor concerned under Article 709 and/or the hospital which hires the doctor under Article 715.

---

31. *See* Robert B. Leflar, *Law and Patient Safety in the United States and Japan*, in *Readings in Comparative Health Law & Bioethics* 124, 126 (Timothy Stoltzfus Jost ed., 2nd ed., Carolina Academic Press 2007).
32. Intention and negligence are provided in the same article and shall have the same result in the text, but there may be some difference in practice concerning the amount of compensation, especially in pain and suffering.

B. Breach of Contract

37. Article 415 of the Civil Code provides that if an obligor fails to perform his/her duty consistent with the purpose of its obligation, the obligee shall be entitled to demand damages arising from such failure, and that the same shall apply to cases when it has become impossible to perform due to reasons attributable to the obligor. The requirements are:

(1) failure or incompleteness of the performance;
(2) responsibility of the obligor; and
(3) damage and causation.

Unlike in torts, the defendant would be the hospital, not the doctor concerned. This is because doctors are employees of hospitals, and a contract is made between a patient and a hospital. So patients may not sue the individual doctor as a defendant in a breach-of-contract scheme.

The plaintiff has the burden of proof on items (1) and (3), and the defendant has the burden on (2). Therefore, in order to escape liability, the defendant hospital must prove, that is, convince the court, that it has no responsibility for the adverse result. This responsibility is understood to be almost the same as negligence, so it was said that a breach-of-contract scheme was advantageous in that the plaintiff does not have the burden of proof that the defendant was negligent. We will return to this point later.

Extinctive prescription is ten years in general, and twenty years in cases of harm to human life and body (Article 167) from the point when it became possible to exercise the right (Article 166, and if the plaintiff knows that he/she has a right, they are shortened to five years).

C. Negligence and Causation

38. However, it is widely understood that these two schemes are practically the same (lawyers for the plaintiff often claim both counts). This is because the decision of incompleteness involves that of negligence. We have the distinction of *obligation de moyens* and *obligation de résultat*, and the obligation of the hospital and/or doctor arising from a medical contract is construed as the former. The content of the obligation is to perform medical practice according to the standard, and the plaintiff has to prove the deviation from the standard, which is to prove negligence.

Abstractly, doctors have the highest duty to avoid risk, for they control human life and health (15 Minshu 244 (Sup. Ct., 16 February 1961)).[33] However, this duty

33. A patient who had surgery in a government-run hospital got syphilis through transfusion, and she sued the government as an employer of her attending doctor. At that time sales of blood was allowed, and the blood used in her surgery was derived from an 'occupational seller' of his own blood. The doctor asked him only whether he was healthy or not (he replied in the affirmative), but he had had intercourse with a prostitute about two weeks before the transfusion. The patient alleged that if the doctor had asked more, the donor might have confessed that intercourse, and she would not have

of care is difficult to prove in particular cases. 'Medical standard as practice'[34] was proposed by a doctor of forensic medicine and has been accepted by the courts. This standard shall be distinguished from mere practice among ordinary doctors because it is a normative one.[35]

A generalist has the same duty of care in that he/she should transfer the patient to a relevant specialist.[36] Heightened standards apply to large hospitals.[37]

In theory, as stated above, the plaintiff has the burden of proof of negligence in both torts and breach of contract. Courts, sometimes, lower or shift the burden of proof to the defendant using presumption. One classic example is flare after injection, which is thought to be the result of either poor quality of the content of the injection or failure of the doctor to disinfect his/her hands. Both imply the doctor's negligence. The Supreme Court decided that failure to comply with the requirements on the label affixed to the drug was presumed to be negligence except if there is a due reason for non-compliance.[38]

39. On causation, the standard of proof is 'high probability', and the Supreme Court said that a finding of causation is a matter of law and that it suffices if an ordinary man has no question on its probability.[39] It might be said that in some cases, courts factually shift the burden of proof on causation, especially in the case of Hepatitis B infection after vaccination.[40]

---

received the blood from him. The courts decided that the doctor had been negligent in not asking more concrete questions of the donor. Some legal scholars understood that this is, in fact, absolute liability, a position which the Civil Code does not take.

34. The proposer of this notion distinguished it with 'medical standard in academic field'. *See* Toyoji Matsukura, *Igaku To Horitsu No Aida* 131 (1977).
35. 50 Minshu 1 (Sup. Ct., 23 Jan. 1996). A drop in blood pressure and cardiac arrest occurred during a surgery for appendicitis. The label on the anaesthetic instructed doctors to check blood pressure every two minutes, but the defendant doctor told the nurse to check it every five minutes and such was the ordinary practice at that time. The Supreme Court held that negligence was presumed when there was a deviation from instructions on the affixed label without due reason for such deviation. *See* on presumption below.
36. 57 Minshu 1466 (Sup. Ct., 11 Nov. 2005). *See also*, Iryokagominjisaibanreishu 158 (Tokyo App. Ct., 27 May 1966).
37. 49 Minshu 1499 (Sup. Ct., 9 Jun. 1995). This was a Retinopathy of Prematurity (ROP) case. The plaintiff was born as a thirty-one-week and 1,508-gram premature baby in 1974. Laser photocoagulation was not common at that time (a report funded by the Ministry of Health was issued in 1975), and previous judgments held that laser photocoagulation in ROP became a standard after publication of the report. In this case the defendant hospital was a large hospital situated in an urban area, and the Supreme Court demanded that the lower court decide whether the defendant hospital had been negligent based on the nature and surroundings of the hospital, speciality of doctors and expectation of patients.
38. 50 Minshu 1 (Sup. Ct., 23 Jan. 1996) above.
39. 29 Minshu 1417 (Sup. Ct., 24 Oct. 1975).
40. 60 Minshu 1997 (Sup. Ct., 16 Jun. 2006).

D. Rights and Legally Protected Interests

1. General Explanation

40. Japanese civil law does not require actual damage even in negligence, so emotional distress becomes subject to compensation. Not only life and health but more abstract interests such as the right to have enough information and to self-determination are protected in both torts and contract. Besides the following 'some possibility' rule, the Supreme Court has affirmed the validity of interests,[41] including:

(1) deciding whether to have surgery with transfusion;[42]
(2) choosing to have breast conservative therapy at another hospital;[43]
(3) letting family members know one's diagnosis of end-stage cancer so that the patient can receive more passionate care from family members;[44] and
(4) knowing the risk of natural birth in order to decide whether to have a natural birth or a Caesarean section.[45]

2. Duty to Provide Information to the Patient

41. As is often the case in other countries, the 'informed consent' doctrine was introduced from the US and had been easing the burden of proof for the plaintiff patient because he/she does not have to prove negligence of the diagnosis or medical procedure itself; it may suffice for the plaintiff to prove the fact of lack of informed consent, which is much easier for the plaintiff to prove because the fact is clear for him/her.

In the past, the Supreme Court[46] held that the nature of procedure and risks associated with the procedure was sufficient and rejected plaintiff's argument that more information, that is, present condition and its cause, improvement by the procedure, prognosis without the procedure, unforeseeable risk and necessary preparation, should be provided. But courts have widened the physicians' duty of providing information to patients. Recent decisions, generally, require diagnosis, nature and

---

41. *See* 1401 Saibanshojiho 14 (Sup. Ct., 8 Dec. 2005) (Yokoo and Izumi JJ., dissenting).
42. 54 Minshu 583 (Sup. Ct., 29 Feb. 2000) (Jehovah's Witnesses).
43. 55 Minshu 1154 (Sup. Ct., 27 Nov. 2001). It should be noted that breast conservative therapy was not common in Japan when the incident occurred (1991).
44. 1083 Hanreijihou 28 (Sup. Ct., 24 Sep. 2002). It should be added that disclosure of diagnosis (especially of cancer) to the patient has been rare, and disclosure to family members has been common. In this judgment, the court ordered the defendant hospital to search and find suitable family members.
45. 1912 Hanreijihou 16 (Sup. Ct., 8 Sep. 2005).
46. 1011 Hanreijihou 54 (Sup. Ct., 19 Jun. 1981). It should be noted that this was an emergency case, and the doctor told the 10 year-old patient's parents that a transfusion would be needed and gave them the option of entering the operating room (the parents refused, but an uncle of the patient attended). Moreover, the lower court discussed whether more information should have been provided and held in the negative because it might have caused a delay in the operation and anxiety for the patient/parents; the Supreme Court approved that decision.

reason of proposed procedure, the risk associated with the procedure, the prospect of success of the procedure and prognosis without the procedure, and alternatives, some of which were denied in the above judgment.

42. A problem in informed consent is whether there is legal causation between lack of information and the negative result. As an example, let us examine two hypothetical cases. In both cases, doctors gave inadequate information about the procedure. The one difference is that the patient in case A would not have consented to the procedure had he/she been given precise information, whereas the patient in case B would have so consented. Courts would hold that there is legal causation between the doctor's negligence and the bad result in case A, whereas they would not approve causation in case B and would only permit damages for pain and suffering (loss of a chance for self-determination). Actually, courts have decided in this manner in cases of AVM (Arteriovenous Malformation). In one case, a district court approved compensation for damages resulting from serious disability,[47] whereas another court approved only emotional damages.[48]

43. Furthermore, with regard to damage and causation, when the procedure itself is successful, the sole negative result is emotional distress. In such cases, the courts (only) grant less compensation based on emotional damages. For example, a patient who was a member of Jehovah's Witnesses refused a transfusion, but the doctor performed a transfusion during the surgery anyway. Courts granted compensation of JPY 500,000 based on doctor's failure to disclose his/her intent of possible transfusion.[49]

3. To Whom Do Doctors Have a Duty?

44. It is clear that doctors have a duty to the patients whom they treat. Courts admit, however, that doctors have a duty to family members in some cases. For example, a doctor saw a patient with lung cancer and thought that the patient was too old and too terminal to receive an explanation of the diagnosis. His wife was old too and had heart failure, so she could not come to the hospital. The doctor failed to tell either the patient or the family members about the diagnosis. After the

---

47. 835 Hanreitaimuzu 275 (Niigata Dist. Ct., 10 Feb. 1994). The court granted compensation of costs for nursing (until average life expectancy), remodelling of the house, and loss of profit. Total amount was more than JPY 85 million.
48. 1463 Hanreijihou 102 (Tokyo Dist. Ct., 31 Aug. 1992). The court found that doctors had explained to the patient that the risk of the procedure was similar to that of an airplane accident but that the patient would have consented to the procedure even if she had had precise information. Thus, the court only admitted emotional damages resulting from loss of the chance to self-determination based on enough information and granted compensation of JPY 6 million. A neurosurgeon critiqued this decision, arguing that in the Niigata case, where doctors saved the life of the patient (although she suffered a serious disability), courts granted much more compensation than in the Tokyo case, where the patient died. But, legally, this difference was based on causation and amount of damages (it may be possible that greater monetary loss results from serious disability (until the patient dies) than from the death of the patient).
49. 54 Minshu 583 (Sup. Ct., 29 Feb. 2000) above.

patient died, the child of the patient sued the doctor, claiming that had she been told of the diagnosis, she might have provided compassionate care to the patient. The court approved the plaintiff's claim, holding that the doctor had the additional contractual duty to find the family member(s) and explain the diagnosis when he/she decided it was not proper to explain the diagnosis to the patient.[50]

In another example, a doctor who treated a child with a rare genetic disease (Pelizaeus-Merzbacher disease) was asked by the parents about the penetration of the disease. The doctor (negligently) explained that the disease would not occur in a future child, so the parents decided to have another child, who was born with the same disease. Would the doctor be liable to the parents or to the newborn? The district court[51] and appellate court[52] held that, generally, doctors do not have a duty other than to the patient, but when the doctor offered advice, he/she had an obligation to offer a medically precise explanation.

45. This duty to family members would involve the explanation of the cause of death to surviving relatives. In one case, doctors missed the diagnosis and explained the cause of death incorrectly (choking by aspiration). In a malpractice suit, the actual cause of death was proved by an expert witness to be heart failure. The court[53] held that doctors have an additional duty to the surviving relatives to explain the cause of death because the Civil Code provides for the duty to report the details when a contract of entrusting was ended (Article 645) and because only attending doctors might explain the cause of death. The courts also said that, although this duty should not be so strict because it is not the core duty of the contract when doctors incorrectly explain a cause of death based on insufficient knowledge, they should be liable in torts.

A court did not grant compensation when doctors did not ask the relatives about a hospital post-mortem examination (but they explained the cause of death).[54] Recently, another court held that the duty of explanation to the family members

50. 1083 Hanreijihou 28 (Sup. Ct., 24 Sep. 2002).
51. 1832 Hanreijihou 141 (Tokyo Dis. Ct., 25 Apr. 2003).
52. Not reported (Tokyo Appellate Ct., 27 Jan. 2005). It should be noted that the court granted compensation not only for emotional distress but also for economic damages resulting from nursing costs and remodelling of the house. As stated below, Japanese courts have not granted economic damages in wrongful birth/life cases because to grant such damages is to see the child as a damage. The court stated, however, that the damages were granted based on the burden of the parents, not based on the existence of the child itself. It might be said that in wrongful birth/life actions, the difference is live birth with a disability and abortion, which has ethical issues, but in this case, the difference is live birth with a disability and success of contraception, which has fewer problematic issues, and the court can easily grant the result.
53. 814 Hanreitaimuzu 202 (Hiroshima Dist. Ct., 21 Dec. 1992). *See also*, Yutaka Tejima, *Recent Developments Concerning a Doctor's Legal Duty of Explanation after Medical Treatment in Japan*, 40 Kobe U. L. Rev. 87 (2006).
54. 1646 Hanreijihou 64 (Tokyo App. Ct., 25 Feb. 1999). As discussed below, the autopsy system is very poor in Japan, and unnatural death in hospitals is rarely subject to a coroner's post-mortem examination. But there have been new systems in some areas that do post-mortem examinations after deaths that occur during medical care. *See* www.med-model.jp/.

should be included in the medical contract, so that family members would have an interest in finding out the cause of death.[55]

4. Loss of Chance

46. Another point in this area has arisen in terms of easing the burden of proof of the plaintiff. As mentioned above, the plaintiff must persuade the court that there is 'high probability' of a correlation between the defendant's negligence and the negative result, such as the patient's death. But in practice, the plaintiff often does not have enough proof (one reason is that the rate for autopsy is very low in Japan. *See* Part II, Chapter 3 §6). Lawyers for the plaintiffs have proposed that there should be new factors such as 'to have a proper diagnosis and treatment', and some lower courts have approved of this idea. The Supreme Court admits that where there is some possibility of avoiding the negative result had the defendant acted properly (*conditio sine qua non*), some compensation should be granted even when there is not a high probability. For example, a patient suffering myocardial infarction was rushed to a hospital, but the doctor negligently missed the diagnosis, and the patient died. In this case, there was no causation between the negligence and the negative result (i.e., there was no 'high probability' that the patient would have lived had the doctor made a proper diagnosis and provided proper treatment) but there was some possibility of avoiding the negative result. The court demanded that the doctor/ hospital pay compensation for the emotional distress of the patient.[56]

E. The Amount of Compensation

47. Article 416 of the Civil Code provides that compensation is granted for the loss which would generally occur (general loss), and which the person concerned foresaw or might have foreseen (special loss). Articles 417 and 722 provide that compensation be paid in money. The contents of the compensation are:

(1) economic damages caused directly by the incident and via loss of profit; and
(2) emotional damages.

55. 1880 Hanreijihou 72 (Tokyo App. Ct., 30 Sep. 2005). In this case, the negligence of a hospital staff member (a nurse) was quite clear, but doctors explained the cause of death incorrectly. Police investigated this malpractice, and the director and attending doctor were convicted under Art. 21 of the Doctors Act (previously discussed in Part II §1). The court only needed to say that an incorrect explanation by intention/negligence may result in liability for compensation. The rationale of the judgment was too generalized; the court said that doctors have a duty to explain to family members when it is not possible to explain to the patient, for example, when the patient is unconscious or after the patient dies. But it seems that the rationale for an unconscious patient and a dead patient should be different, for the former is based on substituted judgment and/or the best interest of the patient, while the latter is for the inherent interest of the surviving relatives.

56. 54 Minshu 2574 (Sup. Ct., 22 Sep. 2000). The Supreme Court admits this theory not only in death cases but also in a severe damage case; 57 Minshu 1466 (Sup. Ct., 11 Nov. 2001) (severe brain damage and disability after acute encephalopathy).

In theory, the plaintiff should prove the amount of damages, but the Civil Procedure Act provides that courts may grant an appropriate amount of compensation without such proof (Article 248).

In 1985, Ooita District Court[57] granted more than JPY 300 million (about USD 3 million) compensation in a case of Endoscopic Retrograde Cholangiopancreatography to an owner of a newspaper company. This judgment was remanded by the appellate court,[58] but the ultimate award was still more than JPY 100 million.

As described above, emotional damages are granted in negligence, and they often become the 'cushion' of economic damages. For example, as described below, courts seldom grant economic damages in wrongful birth cases, but the amounts awarded for emotional damages are relatively high (in millions), whereas transfusion against the patients' will amounts to only a half million.[59]

III. Criminal Liability

48. There are two categories of criminal liability in the medical field: intentional homicide, including homicide with the victim's consent and assisted suicide; and negligent, where death or injury is caused by negligence.

A. *Homicide*

49. The Japanese Criminal Code provides that those who kill shall be sentenced to the death penalty, indefinite term imprisonment or imprisonment of not less than five years (Article 199). It also provides that those who incite or aid another person to commit suicide, or those who kill another person with his/her consent, shall be sentenced to imprisonment of not less than six months and not more than seven years (Article 202). The Supreme Court admitted that withdrawal of treatment might constitute homicide. We will discuss this matter in Part II, Chapter 2, §3 below.

B. *Causing Death or Injury by Negligence*

50. Generally, those who cause injury to another by negligence shall be sentenced to a fine of not more than JPY 300,000, and those who cause death shall be sentenced to a fine of not more than JPY 500,000. If the injury or death occurs during a social activity, or the result is caused by gross negligence, the person shall be sentenced to imprisonment of not more than five years or a fine of not more than

57. 1180 Hanreijihou 7.
58. 37 Shoumugeppou 909.
59. 54 Minshu 583 (Sup. Ct., 29 Feb. 2000) above.

JPY 1 million (Article 211). Providing medical care is considered a social activity,[60] so doctors and other medical personnel may be punished by imprisonment without suspension in theory; of course, almost all cases are sentenced with a stay of execution.[61]

IV. Alternative Dispute Resolution and Other No-Fault Compensation Schemes

A. *No-Fault Compensation on Yakugai*

51. We have experienced large-scale 'Yakugai' (unexpected adverse drug reactions), for example, with thalidomide; with quinoform, which was developed as a disinfectant but was used in Japan for minor intestinal disorders and caused Subacute Myelo-Optico-Neuropathy(SMON); with chloroquine, a drug for the treatment of malaria but was widely used in Japan for chronic nephritis and rheumatism and caused chloroquine retinopathy; and with a coagulant that caused Acquired Immune Deficiency Syndrome (AIDS) in many haemophilia patients. In 1980, as a requirement in an arbitration of a SMON suit, a public no-fault compensation system was established. This system, now administered by the government drug agency Pharmaceuticals and Medical Device Agency,[62] is maintained by payments from pharmaceutical companies according to their proportion of sales and the amount of payment from the system in the previous year. A patient who suffers adverse side effects from a drug may apply for compensation. A patient does not need to prove the negligence/defect of the drug nor prove the causation. He/she only needs to exhibit a certificate from a doctor that states he/she took the drug. Determination of causation is considered in an MHLW committee. The amount of compensation is provided in administrative regulations;[63] for example, when a patient needs medical care, the fee (co-payment of the health insurance) is covered, and JPY 35,800 is paid per month as a treatment benefit. If the patient suffers a severe disability, around JPY 2 million is paid per year, and if he/she dies, about JPY 7 million is paid initially and around JPY 2 million will be paid per year for ten years.

---

60. Whether defendant's act constitutes a 'social activity' is judged by the subjective purpose of the defendant, that is, whether he/she would repeat the act in a social context. Whether the act is legal or not is irrelevant. So a nurse's mistake concerning an intravenous injection was judged as 'negligence in social activity', even when an IV injection by nurses was prohibited by an MHLW circular (15 Sep. 1951, repealed by a circular on 30 Sep. 2004). *See* 7 Keishu 2608 (Sup. Ct., 22 Dec. 1953).
61. Recently a doctor was sentenced to ten months' imprisonment (without suspension) for a nurse's mistake concerning administration of a drug (not reported, Osaka App. Ct., 2 Feb. 2006).
62. www.pmda.go.jp/english/services/healtheffect/outline.html.
63. http://law.e-gov.go.jp/htmldata/H16/H16SE083.html.

B. No-Fault Compensation on Birth Defects

52. As of January 2009, some birth defects became subject to no-fault compensation. It is generally believed that many doctors in obstetrics and gynaecology are afraid of malpractice suits and police investigations that may include arrest, and as a result, some stop attending to births,[64] making it is difficult for women/couples to find hospitals and clinics. To ease these difficulties for both doctors and the general public, hospitals and clinics (and midwives) are encouraged to purchase insurance to cover cerebral paralysis incurred during delivery (so congenital cerebral paralysis would not be compensated). The requirement for collecting insurance is either: (1) birth weight of 2,000 grams or more and at least thirty-three weeks of gestation, or (2) at least twenty-eight weeks of gestation and some additional requirements,[65] and as described above, congenital cerebral paralysis may not be compensated. This system is private and in that hospitals and clinics voluntarily purchase private insurance, but the MHLW negotiated with insurance companies, and ultimately the premium will be paid by national health insurance; if a hospital or a clinic pays the premium (JPY 30,000 per delivery), it may charge the same amount of money to the mother, and if she pays, national insurance will compensate the mother as well.[66]

C. Complaints from Patients

53. In the late 1990s and into the twenty-first century, many malpractice accidents, such as the mistaken identity of patients, occurred, and the MHLW set up a scheme for patient safety. As a result, every prefecture must have an officer or officers staffing a patient safety support centre (Iryou Anzen Shien Sentaa) where they can hear patients' complaints.[67] Also, prefectural branches of the JMA have consultation offices. Further, hospitals are encouraged to have a consultation room, which is one of the requirements of 'additional reimbursement for medical safety' in health insurance.[68] In fact, some hospitals employ victims and/or surviving relatives of victims of malpractice as mediators or as advocates between patients and hospital personnel.

---

64. For a long time, private clinics were used mainly for normal births (including Caesarean sections), and large hospitals for abnormal births, such as multiple pregnancy and low-birth-weight. But doctors running the clinics are getting old and some have retired, and young doctors tend not to choose ob/gyn as their speciality, so the number of both clinics and hospitals for childbirth has been decreasing. The problem is reported in 'Birth Refugees' (Osan Nan'min).
65. www.sanka-hp.jcqhc.or.jp/.
66. Generally, national health insurance provides medical care to the insured through its contract with hospitals and physicians, but in obstetrics, national health insurance only pays a fixed amount (JPY 350,000) to the insured regardless of actual doctor/hospital fee.
67. Medical Care Act, Arts 6–11. Details are provided at www.anzen-shien.jp/.
68. JPY 850 (if the hospital has full-time workers for only medical safety) or 350 (if it has full-time workers for medical safety who may do other work) is paid per hospitalization of patient.

Part II. The Physician-Patient Relationship

Chapter 1. General Description

§1. Rights and Duties of Patients and Physicians

I. Rights of Patients Generally

54. In the 1990s, some rights of patients were added to the Medical Care Act. Article 1 provides that one of the purposes of the Act is to protect the interests of patients by helping them choose appropriately, and Article 1-2 provides that medical care should be based on respect for life and the dignity of the individual and on mutual trust between medical providers (doctor, dentist, pharmacist, nurse and so on) and patient. Article 1-4 requires providers to do their best to provide high-quality and proper care and appropriate explanations to patients. As these rights are abstract and are provided as a duty of endeavour, however, no judgment has been based on those provisions.

It should be noted that, as described above, courts have recognized some kinds of rights in malpractice cases, independent from these statutory ones, for example, the right to know about medical procedures and the right to self-determination.

II. Duty of Physicians Generally

55. The Doctors Act provides that practising doctors have to provide care to patients who seek their care (Article 19). This provision has been understood as a 'duty in public law' (duty to the government)[69] or as an ethical duty[70] because it has no penalty. But courts have used this provision as a basis of negligence because a breach of (public law) duty may be construed as presumed negligence, so the defendant doctor and hospital have to rebut the presumption.[71]

Other duties in the Doctors Act are:

69. Tatsukichi Minobe, *Gyouseihou Kara Mitaru Ishi Fuoushou Mondai (1)–(4)*, Houritsu Shimbun 1047–1050 (1915). It may be worth noting that Minobe was a professor of administrative law.
70. Koichi Bai, *Iji Hougaku Eno Ayumi* 307 (1970).
71. 1458 Hanreijihou 127 (Kobe Dist. Ct., 30 Jun. 1996). It should be noted that not only the doctor but also the hospital is presumed to be negligent.

- to see the patient by himself/herself and to issue a medical certificate or death certificate on request (Articles 19, 20);
- to notify the police within twenty-four hours when he/she finds abnormalities in a dead body (Article 21);
- to provide prescriptions (with some exceptions; *see* Part III §1) (Article 22);
- to advise on health matters including what should be done at home (Article 23); and
- to write a medical chart (to be kept for at least five years by the director of the clinic or hospital) (Article 24).

Violation of the requirements in Articles 20–22 and 24 may result in a penalty of not more than JPY 500,000 (Article 33-2), which used to be rare. Nowadays, the duty provided in Article 21 (to notify the police) has been the subject of public debate as to whether the death of a patient from malpractice should be reported or not.[72]

56. In the *Toritsu Hiroo Byouin* (Tokyo Metropolitan Hiroo Hospital) case, a nurse misunderstood hibitane (antiseptic) as heparin (anticoagulant) and provided the former intravenously. The patient died. It was a national holiday, so the next morning, the administrator of the hospital held a committee meeting and consulted with the Office of Hospital Management of Tokyo's Metropolitan Office as to whether to report the death to the police or not, and twenty-four hours had passed. In this case, the administrator of the hospital (a physician) was prosecuted on counts of letting the attending doctor falsify the death certificate as if the patient had died of cardiac arrest, and of failing to notify the police about the abnormal death.

The defendant administrator argued that the duty to notify was against Article 38 of the Japanese Constitution, which prohibits self-incrimination and guarantees the right to remain silent in a criminal procedure, but the Supreme Court decided[73] that there should be some reasonable limit to such right for doctors because of the nature of the licence of doctors and the strong public interest involved.

57. In all malpractice cases, death is 'abnormal', so the police use this provision as a clue in their investigation.[74] In one malpractice case, in which a woman in labour died from loss of blood caused by placenta accreta, the attending doctor was arrested and accused not only of causing death by negligence but also of not reporting the death to the police.[75]

Medical associations such as the Japan Surgery Society oppose this provision because, they say, fatal complications are unavoidable in some cases, and police investigations harass doctors. Ten such associations jointly issued a set of guidelines which provides that not only death but also severe injury should be reported to

72. *See* Norio Higuchi, *Article 21 of the Medical Practitioners Law*, 51 Jap. Med. Assoc. J. 258–261 (2008).
73. 58 Keishu 247 (Sup. Ct., 13 Apr. 2004).
74. It should be noted that confession has great importance in Japanese criminal procedure generally, and in malpractice cases, in which there is scarce physical evidence and negligence is often based on the confession of the defendant doctor, its importance is greater than in ordinary criminal cases.
75. The doctor was found not guilty (2295 Hanreijihou 6, Fukushima Dist. Ct., 20 Aug. 2008).

police only if the results are caused by negligence. This would mean that they still think doctors need not report death caused by unavoidable complications. On the other hand, the Japanese Society of Legal Medicine holds that all unnatural deaths should be reported to the police.[76] Recent amendment of Medical Care Act provides the duty of administrators of hospitals and clinics to report 'unexpected death' to the designated 'the Center for Medical Accident Investigation/Support' (Articles 6–10(1)), to explain to the surviving family members as defined by the regulations (Articles 6–10(2)) and to investigate the cause of accidents (Articles 6–11).

III. The Right to Consent and Information

58. As described above, medical intervention without consent would be unlawful, and courts have granted compensation in such cases. The first such court decision was issued in 1971. A woman consented to have surgery on her right breast, but during the surgery, doctors removed both breasts. The Tokyo District Court[77] granted her claim, saying that generally, doctors should get a patient's consent to surgery, besides the request of treatment, and that surgery without consent is an unlawful intervention. Later, the need for consent became undisputable, and the subject of discussion moved to the content of the information as a prerequisite of consent. In Japan, as provided above, liabilities from intentional tort and negligence are not distinguished, so whether patients have – and courts protect – the integrity of body or the right to have enough information is not clear. The Supreme Court only says that patients have a right to decision-making as a personal right (Persönlichkeitsrecht)[78] and that doctors have a duty to give patients a chance to decide based on adequate information.[79] Whether courts admit 'the right to refuse treatment' is unclear;[80] as described below in euthanasia, lower courts did not grant, and the Supreme Court would not grant, 'the right to die' and 'the right to kill oneself' but only 'the right to choose how to live ... in the final stage of life' (so courts restricted death with dignity only when the patient was in a terminal stage). Further, the Penal Code prohibits both assisting the suicide of another and killing another with the victim's consent (Article 202). And generally, killing is done by an act, but it may also be done by omission when the person has a duty to act. It would follow that the problem is whether the refusal of the patient (and other requirements) discharges the

76. These opinions of medical associations may be found at the MHLW website, www.mhlw.go.jp/shingi/2007/04/dl/s0420-11c_05.pdf.
77. 22 Kaminshuu 626 (Tokyo Dist. Ct., 19 May 1971). Before this judgment, a district court granted patient's claim, stating that doctors might provide surgery without the patient's consent only when the ordinary doctor thought it necessary to cure the patient. Not reported (Nagasaki Dist. Ct., Sasebo Branch, 28 May 1930).
78. 54 Minshu 583 (Sup. Ct., 29 Feb. 2000) (Jehovah's Witnesses).
79. 1912 Hanreijihou 16 (Sup. Ct., 8 Sep. 2005) above.
80. But a court declared that the refusal of surgery does not constitute a tort to the parents of the patient. In this case, the parents claimed that they were at risk of not being supported by their son if he refused the proposed surgery (he would soon die), and demanded that the court issue a temporary declaratory judgment that they had the right to consent on behalf of their son. The court rejected the claim, saying that the refusal was firmly rooted to his faith and the parents' interest was not strong enough to render the refusal unlawful. 1180 Hanreijihou 113 (Ooita Dist. Ct., 2 Dec. 1985).

duty of the physician to provide treatment. A district court held that the agreement to provide surgery without transfusion was against public order and good morals, and was, therefore, null and void (Article 90 of the Civil Code),[81] although the upper courts reversed and remanded the judgment.[82]

59. Whether a patient has a right to access to information on his/her medical chart was once highly disputed, but an Act on the protection of personal information was enacted in 2003, and medical information was not excluded (furthermore, medical history is protected as 'sensitive personal information' (Article 2(2)). Now, it is a general perception that patients have a right to access their medical information[83] and to decide who may use it and how it is to be used.

60. The Act exempts research use of (identifiable) health information if the use is for research purposes and if the user belongs to an academic institution such as a university (Article 50).[84] In spite of the exemption, governmental guidelines postulate researchers to follow the requirements in the guidelines (*see* paragraph 118 below). Regional cancer registration was not provided in statutes directly and, therefore, was not mandated (some prefecture did not have regional cancer registration) until recently.[85] In December 2013, the National Cancer Registration Act was passed, which will be effective in 2016. The Act provides that the Minister of HLW has a responsibility to establish the National Cancer Database (Article 5); the administrators of any hospital must report information to the Minister through the governor of prefectures about cancer patients who were diagnosed in the hospital (Article 6: report from the administrators of medical clinics is voluntary), and the mayors of cities and villages must send a copy of death registration to regional public health offices (Article 11). The Act permits the data to be kept identifiable while identification is needed (it would be some years after the patient dies), and after that, the data should be anonymized (Article 15).

81. 44 Shoumugeppou 315 (Tokyo Dist. Ct., 12 May 1997).
82. 54 Minshu 583 (Sup. Ct., 29 Feb. 2000) above.
83. Once a court rejected a claim from patients who based their right on the Act. It held that the Act does not provide for a private right of action through court decision and that the data subject (in this case, a patient) should claim to the data holder according to the Act (1978 Hanreijihou 27 (Tokyo Dist. Ct., 27 Jun. 2007)). Amendment to the Act in 2015 provides the right to disclose one's information by the data holder (Art. 28).
84. *See* Shin Utsugi, Sumio Sugano & Shohei Yonemoto (eds), *Jintai no Kojin Jouhou* (Nihon Hyouron Sha 2004) and Shigekoto Kaihara & Norio Higuchi (eds), *Iryou no Kojinjouhou to Security* (2nd ed., Yuuhikaku 2005).
85. http://www.jacr.info/eng/index.html.

IV. Confidentiality

61. The Penal Code requires confidentiality from doctors, dentists, midwives and pharmacists unless there is the due reason (Article 134; under penalty of imprisonment of not more than six months or a fine of not more than JPY 100,000).[86] Other medical technicians are not included in the provision, but special statutes, such as the Act on Nurses and Midwives, require confidentiality of nurses and other healthcare technicians (carrying a fine of not more than JPY 500,000, but in the case of nurses, imprisonment of not more than six months or a fine of not more than JPY 100,000). Further, in specific areas, the statute requires confidentiality (with a penalty in the Infectious Disease Protection Act of imprisonment of not more than one year or a fine of not more than JPY 500,000, and in the Mental Health Act, imprisonment of not more than one year or a fine of not more than JPY 1 million).

There are some exceptions; that is, doctors may breach confidentiality when they have a due reason. For example, doctors have a legal duty to inform public health office when they diagnose some kinds of contagious diseases. Doctors in public hospitals (who are public servants) have a duty to inform the police department about a patient's use of illegal drugs. The Supreme Court judged that drug testing based on such notice from the attending doctor is not illegal, so the result of a urine test is competent proof.[87]

86. It is quite rare for a doctor to be prosecuted on this provision. But recently, a doctor was found guilty for letting a journalist read a juvenile's confession during the police investigation for whom he had done forensic psychiatric assessment. 66 Keishu 405 (Sup. Ct., 13 Feb. 2012).
87. 59 Keishu 600 (Sup. Ct., 19 Jul. 2005).

Chapter 2. The Physician-Patient Relationship in Specific Terms

§1. Minor Patient

I. Medical Neglect Cases and the Legal System in Japan

62. It was in 1985 that the famous *Kawasaki* case occurred. It started as a traffic accident when a dump truck hit a 10-year-old boy. The boy was immediately sent to a university hospital with severe fractures and bleeding, but when the doctors explained to the boy's parents, who rushed to the hospital, that the boy needed a transfusion for the operation, they refused to give consent based on their faith as followers of Jehovah's Witnesses. The doctors were not permitted to operate with blood transfusion on the boy, and he died from loss of blood. It is reported that the boy told his father that he wanted to live.[88] There was no court intervention before the operation, but the case attracted much public and academic attention, leading to the guidelines discussed below and to the revision debate on the current child protection laws we will refer to shortly.

A medical neglect case hit the front page of a local newspaper in 2003 when parents of a boy with heart disease refused to give consent to an operation. The child protection agency contacted the parents, but they refused to give consent based on their religious beliefs. The agency temporarily protected the boy, and the head of the agency (hereinafter referred to as the agency) filed a petition to the family court for the termination of parental rights and at the same time, filed a petition for the suspension of parental rights and temporary transfer of the power to consent to the medical treatment to the agency until the final order. The court granted the petition and the boy was operated on and recovered.[89]

63. There were now three reported legal cases on medical neglect before the revision of the Civil Code in 2011. All of them used the same procedure as the case above. One is the refusal of treatment of a neonate in Osaka based on religious belief,[90] another is the refusal of treatment of a neonate with congenital heart disease in Nagoya,[91] and the third is the refusal of treatment of a boy with eye cancer in Tsu.[92]

The Osaka case report does not mention what disease the neonate suffered from, but it had something to do with brain development, and according to the finding of fact, if nothing was done for the child, there was a high likelihood that the condition would lead to developmental retardation and danger to life, while the chances of normal development if the operation were performed were high and the danger posed by the operation was relatively small. So, even if the refusal by the parents

88. Asahi Simbun 7 Jun. 1985.
89. Chunichi Shimbun 10 Aug. 2003.
90. 59-4 Kateisaibangeppou 135 (Osaka family Ct., Kishiwada branch, 15 Feb. 2005).
91. 59-4 Kateisaibangeppou 127 (Nagoya family Ct., 25 Sep. 2006).
92. 62-8 Kateisaibangeppou 83 (Tsu family Ct., 25 Jan. 2008).

was based on religion, the operation was needed to save the life and sound development of the child. As the disease was a progressive one, immediate medical intervention was necessary, so the court ordered the suspension of parental rights and temporarily transferred the power to consent to the medical treatment to the doctor, who is an authority of the disease. According to news reports, after the operation was done successfully, the child protective agency withdrew the petition to terminate parental rights.

The Nagoya case was a refusal of treatment of a child with congenital heart disease based on religious belief. The child needed an operation during infancy and again at age 4 or 5. The child protective agency filed a petition to terminate the parental rights on the ground that it was an abuse of parental rights not to consent to the necessary treatment and at the same time, filed a petition to suspend parental rights and to temporarily transfer the power to consent to the operation until the final order was issued. The court granted the petition based on the following reasons. The child's life was in danger without the operation, but the parents, who are responsible for the custody and care of the child, refused to consent to the needed operation to save the child's life. The reason for refusal was not considered rational, and the child's life would be in danger without the operation. So, the refusal of consent by the parents constituted the abuse of parental rights to the detriment of the child. Accordingly, the suspension of parental rights and the temporary transfer of the power to consent to the operation to a lawyer concerned during the suspension period were ordered.

The Tsu case is about the refusal of treatment to a boy with eye cancer. He needed an emergency operation to remove the right eye, partial surgery on the left eye and also a chemo-therapy. If he underwent that procedure, there is a 90% chance that he would be cured. However, even though his life would be saved, there is a strong likelihood that his eyesight in both eyes would be lost and his parents thought they were not able to consent to his surgery because of that. If he did not undergo the operation, he would be likely to die from the disease within several months. The child protective agency filed a petition to terminate the parental rights on the ground that it was an abuse of parental rights not to consent to the necessary treatment and at the same time, filed a petition to suspend parental rights and transfer the power to consent to the operation temporarily until the final order was issued. The court granted the petition based on the following reasons using the same logic as the Nagoya court. The child's life was in danger without the operation, but the parents, who were responsible for the custody and care of the child, refused to give consent to the needed operation to save the child's life. The attitude of parents was not considered rational, and the child's life would be in danger without the operation. So, the refusal of consent by the parents constituted the abuse of parental rights to the detriment of the child. Accordingly, the suspension of parental rights and the temporary transfer of the power to consent to the operation to a lawyer concerned during the suspension period were ordered.

64. As we can see, the legal cases discussed above all used the same legal method to protect medically neglected children from life-threatening danger. However, if we closely examine the child protection laws in Japan, the law was not used as it was intended and was slightly abused. The courts did their best to save the children's lives, but the child protective law was not sufficient for medical neglect cases. It had been strongly argued that the law needed revision and finally, the Civil Code was revised as we shall see the details below, but before we turn to the revision, we shall see why the law was not sufficient.[93]

Termination of parental rights is provided for in Article 834 of the Civil Code and Child Welfare Act 33-7. However, the termination petition is rarely used because the effect of the termination is grave. Expediently, the agency used a temporary court order suspending parental rights and then transferred the consent power until the final order of termination (actually, not only the consent power but all parental powers are transferred as an effect of the temporary court order), but before the termination order, it withdrew the petition to avoid the grave effect of termination. However, there are two requirements for the petition to suspend parental rights and temporarily transfer the power to consent to someone else: (1) the issue of termination order must be certain and (2) there must be a necessity to file this temporary petition, such as a medical emergency. It seems that life-threatening cases meet both of the requirements on the surface, but as mentioned above, the child protective agencies requested the temporary order, but they withdrew the petition before the final order to avoid the termination of parental rights. Otherwise, the termination order would be issued, and the parents would lose parental rights. The withdrawal is arbitrary if we consider that the merits of the case are the termination order and are the prerequisite of the temporary order. The child protective agencies had to do this because most of the parents were considered fit except for the refusal of treatment. The way the law was used is close to abuse even though it was done out of necessity. It should be revised to provide for the temporary suspension of consent power only, not the termination of all parental rights, to enable saving the lives of children without the threat of termination of parental rights, but the Civil Code is yet to be revised on this point.

As the Ministry of Justice took matters seriously, the Civil Code was revised on the parental rights in 2011, and the revised law took effect the next year. The biggest change concerning medical neglect is that it created the suspension of parental rights in Article 834-2, adding to the termination. If the parents use parental rights so improperly or it is so difficult for them to exercise the rights that would lead to the detriment of child's welfare, the family court is able to order the suspension of parental rights for up to two years. (What's more, the child him/herself is able to petition the court.)

Now, the child protective agencies petition for this suspension of parental rights and the temporary order at the same time to save children from medical neglect. It is reported that there are at least three cases of medical neglect using this article, and according to an MHLW report, there is a case of a Down's syndrome child who needed heart surgery for ventricular septal defect, but his parents refused to consent

93. Masahiro Hojo & Yuko Nagamizu, *Nihon Hou no Genjou to Kadai*, in *Kodomo No Iryou To Hou* 29–71 (Go Koyama & Mariko Tamai eds, 2d ed., Shougakusha 2012).

to the surgery. The child could be operated on with the temporary order and the consent of the head of the child protective facility.[94] This case is reported in 1438 Hanrei Times 250 (Tokyo Family Ct., 29 June 2016) later. Another is a case of refusal of blood transfusion to an infant (petition granted) (1423 Hanrei Times 379 (Tokyo Family Ct., 14 April 2015)). The other is a petition of a 17 years old girl, not only concerned with medical neglect but also with neglect in general (educational and financial abuse is also at issue) (petition granted) (65-6 Kateisaibangeppou 115 (Miyazaki Family Ct., 29 March 2013). According to the 2017 statistics, a petition to terminate parental rights was granted in twenty-eight cases while a petition for the suspension was granted in sixty-seven cases. Among them, the cause of the petition was medical neglect in ten suspension cases and two termination cases.[95]

In the meanwhile, the Child Welfare Act was revised, and a notice was issued on 9 March 2012 by the MHLW that the head of the child protective agency is able to consent to the emergency treatment of a dependent child without parental consent or court order. The Civil Code and the Child Welfare Act has a possibility to be at odds with each other if the practice under the Child Welfare Act is lax because if the attending physician says the child's life or health is in imminent danger and the child needs protection, the agency can avoid the burdensome procedure to convince the child's parents or to file a petition for suspension. Such a situation is easily made arbitrarily, and it would not bring a happy ending to the family the child will live for the rest of childhood, to the relationship between the parents and medical institutions, and to the child protective agency itself, as the parents' right to due process is gravely invaded.

65. In the meantime, five societies (Japan Society of Transfusion and Cell Therapy, Japan Society of Anesthesiologists, Japan Pediatric Society, Japan Society of Obstetrics and Gynaecology and Japan Surgical Society) established and released guidelines concerning the refusal of blood transfusion based on religion on 28 February 2008. The Guidelines provide a way to save the lives of children even when their parents refuse to give consent to a blood transfusion if there is a danger to their lives without the transfusion.[96] The healthcare facilities will respect the essence of the guidelines, but they are also able to change details depending on their ethical beliefs.

When the minor patient is between 15 and 17 years of age, the course of action for the healthcare provider depends on the circumstances, seen here in the following three scenarios:

(1) When the parents refuse to give consent, but the minor patient turns in a written consent document to the healthcare providers, that minor will be given the transfusion.

---

94. http://www.mhlw.go.jp/stf/houdou/2r98520000037b58-att/2r98520000037bau.pdf.

95. Family Division, Secretariat of the Supreme Court of Japan 'Overview of Restriction of Parental Rights Cases and Cases on Article 28 Child Welfare Act' at http://www.courts.go.jp/vcms_lf/2018 0420zigyakugaikyou_h29.pdf.

96. *Japanese Journal of Transfusion and Cell Therapy* 54 (2008): 345–351. www.yuketsu.gr.jp/information/2008/refusal1.pdf (last visited July 2008).

(2) When the parents give consent, but the patient refuses transfusion, the healthcare providers must try to do without the transfusion. In life-threatening circumstances, however, they may transfuse the patient; a written consent document from the parents is needed.
(3) When both the parents and the patient refuse the transfusion, the course of action to be taken is the same as treating a patient 18 years old and up,[97] that is, the healthcare providers respect their wishes if they submit the written medical directives, or if they find it difficult to operate without a transfusion, they advise the parents and patient to go to another healthcare facility that may be able to operate without a transfusion, as soon as possible.

Patients younger than 15 years are not competent to give consent to medical treatment and need to be protected from abuse and neglect, so when both parents refuse to give consent, and it is impossible to provide treatment, the healthcare providers report the case to the child protection agency, and the agency files a petition to terminate or suspend the parental rights while at the same time requesting the temporary suspension of the parental rights and the temporary transfer of consent power to someone else until the final order. Then they will get the consent of that other person. When one of the parents refuses to give consent, the healthcare providers will operate on the patient with the consent of the other parent, in case of an emergency.

II. Medical Decision-Making for Severely Ill Newborns

66. The situations surrounding medical decision-making for severely ill newborns are as follows. The 'Guidelines for Healthcare Providers and Parents to Follow in Determining the Medical Care of Newborns with Severe Disease' were published in 2004 by a research group subsidized by the MHLW. These Guidelines were published because the criteria in determining medical care based on the classification of diseases were much criticized and a new approach underlining procedural justice was needed.[98] The disease-based determination criteria led to stiff and routine determinations rather than, as they should be, ethical struggles. The Guidelines aim to pursue the best interests of the particular child in question in determining the medical treatment of that child and, in that sense, their ideal is commendable.[99]

The Guidelines are as follows:[100]

---

97. The coming of age in Japan is 20 years old now, but after the Legislative Council of Ministry of Justice decided to lower it to 18, the Civil Code was amended and the revision will take effect on 1 Apr. 2022.
98. Masanori Tamura & Mariko Tamai (eds), *Shinseiji Iryou Genba No Seimei Rinri* (Medica Shuppan 2005).
99. Yuko Nagamizu, *Medical Decision-Making for Severely Ill Newborns: What We Can Learn from the Critical Analysis of the Child Abuse Amendments of 1984 and Its Regulations*, 8 Momoyama Hougaku 1–17 (2006).
100. www.saitama-med.ac.jp/kawagoe/link08/link22/guideline.pdf.

(1) All newborns have the right to be protected and to receive appropriate medical care.
(2) Parents have the right and also the obligation to determine the course of their children's medical treatment as caretakers who are responsible for their children's growth and development.
(3) Determination of the course of medical treatment must be based on the best interests of the child.
(4) Parents and healthcare providers must fully discuss all options in the process of making decisions regarding treatment.
(5) Healthcare providers must attempt to establish a trusting relationship with the child's parents and treat them as equal partners in the decision-making process.
(6) Healthcare providers are under an obligation to promptly and accurately provide parents with all information regarding their child's condition and all treatment options and to explain such in a language that can be understood by the parents.
(7) Healthcare providers should have the opportunity to present their opinions and information and to express their opinions concerning the treatment of newborns.
(8) The attending physician should determine the child's prognosis based on the latest medical information available given the child's condition and should consult with physicians of other specialities and healthcare providers of other disciplines as necessary.
(9) Withdrawal or withholding of Life-Sustaining Medical Treatment (hereinafter referred to as LSMT) must be discussed with extreme caution, as it could have irreversible consequences for a child's life. If parents or healthcare providers propose the withdrawal or withholding of LSMT, the 'best interests of the child' must be fully discussed, complying with the principles set forth in Articles (1)–(8) above:
   (a) In considering withdrawal or withholding of LSMT, the exchange of opinions should include as many physicians as possible who are involved in the child's medical treatment.
   (b) In considering withdrawal or withholding of LSMT, it is necessary for physicians to discuss fully with the parents all available options. In doing so, the attending physician must, in the presence of other healthcare team members, listen to the parents' opinions and confirm their intentions.
   (c) When the decision is made to withdraw or withhold LSMT, the following must be documented on the child's medical chart: the reason the decision was judged to be in the best interests of the child, the process of the decision-making, and the content of discussions with the family.
   (d) Even after a decision to withdraw or withhold LSMT is made, medical treatment must be pursued in order to comply with the best interests of the child, and maximum support should be given to the family.
(10) The course of treatment should be able to be altered depending on changes in the child's condition or the wishes of the parents. Healthcare providers must inform parents in advance that they can modify the decision any time they wish.

However, as the Guidelines are not nationally adopted, and they avoid the most difficult ethical question of how to determine the withdrawal and withholding of medical treatment, there are continued news reports that some hospitals withdrew treatment from extremely low-birth-weight infants with severe brain haemorrhage based on the hospital guidelines. Hospitals consider some treatments to be inhumane these days; this trend can be seen from the release of figures from the National Center for Child Health and Development. The centre reported the figures at the Annual Meeting of the Japan Pediatric Society in April 2008.[101] According to the centre, LSMTs such as respirators were withdrawn from thirty children thought to be in cardiopulmonary arrest shortly after obtaining the family's consent from March 2002 to May 2007. Aggressive treatments, such as medication, were withheld from fifty additional children. They were all clinically dying, and the withdrawal and withholding of LSMT were decided and implemented with the consultation of the hospital and with the consent of parents. There are no written consent forms, but the progressions of events are recorded in the medical charts.[102] Following this report, the Japan Pediatric Society decided to establish a working group to make guidelines for its members to follow. The guidelines are based on the ones that we introduced above and other research results.[103] The basic tenets of the guidelines are: (1) not to define the criteria in determining the withdrawal or withholding of medical care to avoid making the determination routine, and (2) to cherish the process to create a relationship so that everyone concerned can consider the best interest of the child in determining the medical care for the child.

§2. Mental Patients

I. Brief History

67. At one time, mental patients were detained in their own homes (Shitaku-kanchi). The Mental Hospitals Act of 1919 provided that the (then) Ministry of Internal Affairs might instruct prefectures to establish public (i.e., run by the prefectures) mental hospitals, but the Act also permitted private mental hospitals to be treated as 'substitutes' for public hospitals. As described above, the Japanese government was hesitant to establish public hospitals, so private hospitals have been the main providers and places of detention.

The care in such private hospitals had been highly criticized nationally and internationally; in one tragic case, a mental patient was killed by a hospital employee in 1984. The government decided to amend the statute. In 1987, the statute was amended and added some provisions to ensure the rights of patients. The statute was amended and renamed 'Seishin Hoken Fukushi Hou' in 1995 and is still in effect.

The average term of hospitalization has been shortened but is still relatively long (almost one year), which means care is provided in hospitals. This is, partly, because

101. www.asahi.com/health/news/TKY200804270123.html?ref=reca.
102. *Ibid.*
103. www.jpeds.or.jp/saisin/saisin_120808.pdf.

the number of beds is relatively large (about 350,000), and so-called normalization is quite difficult because of the scarce resources of society outside the hospitals.

II. Purpose of the Statute and Definition

68. The purpose of the statute is to promote the welfare of patients with mental disorders, as well as the mental health of the nation through:

(1) providing medical care and protection to mental patients;
(2) providing help for patients to return to social life and independence; and
(3) preventing mental diseases and taking other measures to improve the mental health of the nation (Article 1).

To achieve this purpose, the central and local government shall take general measures to improve medical and educational facilities so that people with mental disorders may come back to society, be independent and engage in social activities (Article 2). Furthermore, each nation has a duty to preserve and improve its citizens' mental health and to understand patients with mental disorders (Article 3).

69. 'Mental disorder' is defined very broadly: schizophrenia, acute poisoning and addiction, mental retardation, psychopathic personality and other mental diseases (Article 5).

III. Types and Requirements of Hospitalization

70. The types of hospitalization are:

- voluntary hospitalization (Nin'i Nyuin);
- hospitalization with a family member's consent (Iryou Hogo Nyuin); and
- hospitalization without consent (Sochi Nyuin).

The Act provides that directors of mental hospitals should try to use voluntary hospitalization as much as possible (Article 22-3).

71. In voluntary hospitalization, directors of mental hospitals should notify the patient in writing as to how to demand discharge and rights and duties during hospitalization (Article 22-4(1)). The patient may demand discharge, but the Act permits the director to detain the patient for another seventy-two hours if a doctor with certification confirms that hospitalization is needed for the care and protection of the patient (Article 22-4(3)).

72. If a doctor with certification confirms that the patient has a mental disorder and that voluntary hospitalization is not possible because of the disorder, the director of the hospital may hospitalize the patient with a family member's consent

(Article 33). Furthermore, in some cases, such a patient may be hospitalized without a family member's consent for seventy two hours (Article 33-4).

73. Lastly, hospitalization without consent may occur if two doctors with certification consistently confirm that the patient has a mental disorder and that there is some risk of the patient harming himself/herself or harming others without hospitalization.

The clues of this compulsory hospitalization are:

(1) Anyone may request that the governor of the prefecture allow a mental patient to see a doctor with certification for necessary protection.
(2) A policeman should notify the governor about anyone he/she thinks may be in danger of harming himself/herself or others.
(3) A public prosecutor should notify the governor if he/she decides not to prosecute a suspect who might have a mental disorder or if a judgment was settled (except when the judgment was 'guilty with imprisonment').[104]
(4) A director of a correctional institution who lets a detainee with a mental disorder discharge himself/herself should notify the governor.
(5) A director of a mental hospital who lets a patient discharge himself/herself should notify the governor.

The governor who receives such notifications should let doctors with certification see the patient, and as described above, if two doctors' opinions concur, the governor may issue an order to hospitalize the patient. The requirement of the release is provided by Article 29-4, but 'after-care' is not provided in the act, so after the killing of nineteen mental-handicapped people by a former mental patient, the need for care and information-sharing among local authorities after the release has come to light.

IV. Mental Hospital and Doctor

74. As described above, the Act requires prefectures to establish public mental hospitals (Article 19-7). But the Act also provides that this duty may be postponed if there are appointed private mental hospitals.

In some cases, a doctor needs to be certified by the MHLW as a 'doctor with certification'. The requirements for the certification are:

(1) five years' experience in diagnosis or treatment;

104. In criminal procedure, when a defendant is judged as insane, the court must issue a judgment of 'not guilty' (Penal Code Art. 39). A new statute to detain mental patients in national and prefectural hospitals who committed violent acts was enacted in 2003 and became effective in 2005 www.tulips.tsukuba.ac.jp/dspace/bitstream/2241/104820/1/IJLP_33-1.pdf. In the Act, one who is not prosecuted because of insanity and a prosecuted who is found not guilty because of insanity in case of arson, rape, murder, intentional injury and robbery. In fact, because of the shortage of prefectural hospitals, it is said that the use of the procedure is limited to cases in which the victim dies.

(2) three years' experience in diagnosis or treatment of mental disorders;
(3) experience in the treatment and/or diagnosis of some kind of mental disorder set by regulations; and
(4) attendance at lectures (Article 18).

These are to be revised because the fraudulent application became detected, and eighty-nine doctors were revocated of their certification in 2015.

V. Mental Health Committee

75. Each prefecture shall establish one or more mental health committee(s). A committee consists of five members, including two medical professionals, one legal professional and another professional.

A committee examines reports of hospitalization with a family member's consent; regular reports of involuntary hospitalization (with and without a family member's consent) from the hospital (Article 38-3); and requests for discharge from a patient or caregiver (Article 38-5).

VI. Caregiver

76. The Act (before the amendment in 2013) provided duties of a caregiver to ensure that every patient has appropriate medical care. A caregiver might be a legal guardian, a spouse, a person with parental rights or another family member chosen by the family court (in this order: Article 20). If there was no such person, the mayor of a city becomes the caregiver. The caregiver had the responsibility to let the patient get treatment and to protect the assets of the patient, to coordinate proper medical care with doctors, and to comply with the treating doctor's instructions (Article 22). The Amendment in 2013 abolishes the provision of caregiver, but it is not sure that a family member still has civil liability described below.

VII. Tort Liability Concerning Mental Patients

77. Courts admit that caregivers have a third-party duty to prevent the patient from doing harm to others. At one time, the duty to prevent had been provided in the Act, so courts admitted that the duty might become a legal ground in tort (Civil Code, Article 714).[105] But the duty was repealed from the Act in 1999, and so the

105. The Civil Code provides that the mentally incompetent shall have no responsibility of compensation, and that in this case, those who have a duty to control the person should pay the damage which the victim suffered (Art. 714). Courts have admitted this duty broadly; for example, when a child does something wrong, parents shall be liable except if they can prove they did not fail to supervise or the result would have happened even if not for their lack of supervision (but the court seldom grants such an exemption). Caregivers were treated as those who have such a duty in the Mental Health Act.

standard of care to the third party may be lowered.[106] Recently, the Supreme Court rejected a claim by the railway company to the surviving family members on the ground that the family members had not been negligent (70 Minshu 681 (Sup. Ct., 1 March 2016)), which means family members might have legal duty generally.

78. Furthermore, the hospital shall be liable if the employee is negligent, and there is causation between the negligence and the negative outcome. In one case, a patient who had been hospitalized in the mental ward of a prefectural hospital escaped from the hospital, stole a car and drove to another city, where he killed a man with the intent of burglary. The surviving spouse, children and parents of the victim sued the prefecture, and the courts granted compensation.[107]

§3. Dying Patients

I. Introduction

79. In Japan, there are no special statutes or specific provisions in the Criminal Code on euthanasia. Therefore, the problems of euthanasia are mainly left to the legal interpretation of homicide (Article 199, Criminal Code, where there is no distinction between murder and manslaughter) and homicide with the consent of the victim (Article 202, Criminal Code).

II. Cases of Euthanasia by a Doctor

80. In Japan, there are eight reported cases of euthanasia and borderline euthanasia. In two of those cases, doctors actively ended the lives of the patients.[108]

A. The *Tokai Daigaku University* Case

81. A 58-year-old man was in the hospital because of multiple myeloma. He was in the sixth grade of consciousness (no reaction to pain stimulus) and in critical condition, breathing with difficulty and a loud snore. A young doctor-in-charge of the patient was requested to remove the intravenous drip injection and Foley catheter in order to let the patient pass away naturally. The doctor worried about how to deal with the situation and ordered a nurse to remove the intravenous drip injection and the catheter. Subsequently, the eldest son of the patient told the doctor that it was unbearable for him to hear his father's snore and requested the doctor to make his

106. 1844 Hanreijihou 66 (Tokyo High Ct., 29 Oct. 2003). This was not the caregiver's case, but the plaintiff insisted that the family member who cares for the patient should have the same duty as the caregiver. The courts judged against the plaintiff, and one of the reasons was the repeal of the duty of the caregiver.
107. 1594 Hanreijihou 32 (Sup. Ct., 3 Sep. 1996).
108. *See* Katsunori Kai, *Euthanasia in Japanese Law*, in *Euthanasia in International and Comparative Perspective* 187 (Marc Groenhuijsen & Floris Van Laanen eds, Wolf Legal Publishers 2006).

father comfortable. As a result, the doctor injected twice the normal amount of Diazepam (a sedative drug with a side effect of restraining breathing), but the situation of the patient did not change after an hour. The son made a second request. The doctor injected twice the normal amount of Haloperidol (a psychotropic drug with a side effect of restraining breathing). As the situation still did not change after an hour, the son asked angrily what the doctor was doing, as his father's breathing had remained unchanged and because he wanted to take him home soon. The doctor, feeling pressured, decided to comply with the son's request. He first injected twice the normal amount of verapamil hydrochloride (a drug for an irregular pulse with a side effect of transient cardiac arrest), but the situation did not change. He finally injected 20 millilitres of undiluted Potassium Chloride (KCL), and consequently, the patient died. The court found the doctor guilty of homicide and sentenced him to two years of imprisonment with hard labour with a suspension of the sentence for two years (Article 199, Criminal Code).[109]

This was the first case of a doctor being a defendant, and this judgment is particularly interesting because it presented four requirements for lawful active euthanasia, amending six requirements of the Nagoya High Court.[110]

The new requirements are:

(1) the patient is suffering from unbearable physical pain;
(2) the patient's death is unavoidable and the time of death is imminent;
(3) the doctor tries everything to remove or relieve the patient's physical pain, and there are no alternative measures;
(4) there is an explicit expression of the patient's will to accept the shortening of his/her life.

B. The *Kawasaki Kyodo Byouin Hospital* Case

82. The accused was the doctor-in-charge of the patient (a 58-year-old man) who was in the hospital with brain damage due to hypoxemia without regaining consciousness. She believed that it was better to remove the tube in the trachea before it became infected and to let him breathe naturally in the last moments of his life, so she removed the tube, expecting the patient to die. Contrary to her expectation, he did not die and began breathing with difficulty, bending backwards like a shrimp. When the doctor could not quieten his breathing, she did not want the situation made known to the patient's family. She ordered a nurse to inject a muscle-slackening drug into his veins, which killed him. Incidentally, she explained to the

---

109. 1530 Hanreijihou 28 (Yokohama Dist. Ct., 28 Mar. 1995). *See also*, Timothy Stoltzfus Jost, *Readings in Comparative Health Law & Bioethics* 332 (2nd ed., Carolina Academic Press 2007).

110. 15 Koukeishuu 4 (Nagoya App. Ct., 22 Dec. 1962). The requirements were: (1) The sick person suffers from an incurable disease according to modern medical knowledge and technology and the time of death is imminent. (2) The pain of the sick person is extreme and unbearable. (3) The act must be exclusively performed for the purpose of relieving the death throes of the sick person. (4) There must be an earnest request of the patient when he/she is still clearly conscious and can express his/her wishes. (5) In principle, the act must be done by a doctor. If this is impossible, there should be special efforts to persuade others not to do so. (6) The method must be accepted as ethically appropriate.

patient's family that the patient was 99.9% in a situation of brain death, although no exact determination of brain death had been made. The Yokohama District Court found her guilty of homicide and sentenced her to three years' imprisonment with hard labour with a suspension of the execution for five years.[111] The defendant appealed to the Tokyo Appellate Court, which sentenced her to one and a half years' imprisonment with a suspension of three years (the lightest sentence for murder).[112] She appealed to the Supreme Court arguing that at least the removal of the tube was legal, but the Court rejected her appeal.[113]

As in the *Tokai Daigaku University* case discussed above, there was no explicit expression of the patient to end his life. The issue of this case was whether the doctor's chain of actions was substantially justifiable or not.

83. The Yokohama District Court based its reasoning on the judgment in the *Tokai Daigaku University* case (its preceding decision) and described its logics as follows:

(1) Discontinuance of medical treatment in terminal care is permissible only on the grounds of respect for self-determination of the patient and/or the limit of duty of medical treatment based on a medical decision.
(2) Respect for the patient's right to self-determination does not imply admitting suicide and accepting the right to die. It allows the patient to decide for himself/herself how to live his/her own life and, consequently, to decide how to live or die in the final stage of his/her life.
(3) There should be no prospect of the patient's recovery, and death should be imminent. The patient should understand this, and he/she should still be of sound mind.
(4) The patient must be well-informed and must decide voluntarily. His/her decision must be sincerely expressed.
(5)The doctor must determine the real intention of the patient if he/she cannot directly identify the patient's voluntary self-determination and expression.
(6) In determining the real intention of the patient, it is advisable to study documents in which his/her intentions were recorded (e.g., a living will), and to get statements from family members or other people who are aware of the patient's ideas on life. If in spite of all such efforts the real intention of the patient cannot be identified, the doctor should give priority to the protection of the patient's life, based on the principle of 'in dubio pro vita'. He/she will have to continue applying the most suitable medical measures.
(7) When doctors have exhausted available medical treatments, there is no legal duty to continue or perform treatments considered to be harmful or meaningless medically, even if the patient wants such treatment.
(8) The judgment of the doctor should be persistently limited to the validity of medical treatments, and so on. The doctor may advise the patient how to die,

111. 1185 Hanreitaimuzu 114 (Yokohama Dist. Ct., 25 Mar. 2005).
112. 1237 Hanreitaimuzu 153 (Tokyo App. Ct., 28 Feb. 2007).
113. 2066 Hanreijihou 159 (Sup Ct., 7 Dec. 2009).

but such advice should be limited to a consulting opinion, and, therefore, it is not proper for the doctor to do a valuation on behalf of the patient.

84. On the other hand, the Tokyo Appellate Court deliberated whether the act (and/or omission) of the doctor was justifiable either on patient self-determination or on limitation of doctor's duty, without expressing a general formula (it said that the duty of formulating general requirements should be in the hands of the Parliament), and found that both were lacking in this case. But it found that the doctor had acted on the family's demand (the Yokohama District Court had described this based on the doctor's 'peculiar character'), and it shortened the term of imprisonment.

III. Other Cases and Guidelines

85. In Japan, as presented above, the most controversial problem concerning euthanasia is active euthanasia. In the *Tokai Daigaku University* case, the prosecutor limited the counts to active killing, that is, injection of verapamil hydrochloride and KCL. In the *Kawasaki Kyodo Byouin Hospital* case, although the counts were not only active killing but included removal of the tracheal tube, the main point was the former. Recently, the withdrawal of life-sustaining treatment such as a respirator became the subject of police investigation although no cases have been prosecuted. It is said that doctors are afraid to discontinue treatment because of the risk of a police investigation.

This has created the need for professional guidelines. The Ministry of Health,[114] JMA[115] and three associations[116] issued guidelines. These guidelines are not legally binding, and they have no power to prevent prosecution. In March 2019, the withdrawal of dialysis (and succeeding patient's death) happened and was debated.[117] And in 2019 two doctors assisted ALS patient's suicide and they have been indicted in 2020.[118]

114. https://www.mhlw.go.jp/stf/houdou/0000197665.html.
115. https://www.med.or.jp/doctor/rinri/i_rinri/006612.html.
116. http://www.jaam.jp/html/info/2014/info-20141104_02.htm.
117. https://www.japantimes.co.jp/news/2019/03/08/national/tokyo-hospital-probed-149-cases-halting-dialysis-treatment-death-patient/#.XIXmSXOPt1U. You can see a statement from Japanese Society for Dialysis Therapy on the website: https://www.jsdt.or.jp/info/2565.html (in Japanese).
118. https://www.japantimes.co.jp/news/2020/08/13/national/crime-legal/two-doctors-indicted-terminal-als-patients-medically-assisted-suicide/.

Chapter 3. Specific Activities

§1. Abortion

I. Overview

86. Abortion is prohibited by the Penal Code. Section 214 provides that doctors, midwives, or pharmacists who provide abortions by request or consent of a woman shall be subject to not less than three months' and not more than five years' imprisonment, and if the woman suffered injury or death, not less than six months' and not more than seven years' imprisonment. Providers of non-consensual abortion shall be subject to not less than six months' and not more than seven years' imprisonment (Article 215).

However, abortion has been made lawful by special statute. The Eugenics Protection Act (1948) provided that doctors appointed by a prefectural medical association might provide abortion[119] with the consent of the woman concerned (and her husband, if she has one), when:

(1) continuance of pregnancy might harm the health of the woman by physical (bodily, medical) or economic reason;[120] or
(2) the pregnancy was caused by rape or other conditions under which the woman could not refuse intercourse.

These provisions were succeeded by the current Maternity Protection Act. The number of abortions is officially reported as about 165,000 per year as of 2017, whereas the number of newborns is about 946,000 as of 2017. To avoid abortions in unwanted pregnancy cases, a 'Babyklappe' (baby box) was established in one private hospital. Seventeen babies were 'posted' during the first year, whereas the number of consults from parents was about eighty, including eight cases in which parent(s) later decided to keep the baby and twenty-five cases of adoptions.

---

119. Abortion is defined as the excretion of a non-viable foetus. Concerning the 'non-viable' requirement, there is no provision of the gestation weeks (i.e., until when abortion may be legal) in the Act. A Ministry of Health circular provides that abortion is lawful before twenty-two weeks of gestation, and courts abide by this directive (467 Hanreitaimuzu 175 (Naha Dist. Ct (Ishigakijima branch), 15 Mar. 1982)). Furthermore, concerning 'excretion', there is a question whether killing foetus(es) by injection of KCL in the mother's womb, which is needed in case of multiple pregnancy, especially in vitro fertilization and embryo transfer (IVF-ET), is lawful or not. The Penal Code's prohibition may include the killing of the foetus in the uterus (though traditionally the courts defined excretion in the same way as abortion in the Eugenics Protection Act and the Maternity Protection Act). As stated above, the Maternity Protection Act only permits excretion, so, strictly speaking, in utero killing is not lawful under this Act.
120. This 'economical reason' was added in 1949.

II. Abortion Based on (Risk of) Foetal Abnormality and Disease/Disability

87. It should be noted that there is no provision concerning Rubella defects. But doctors rarely ask a woman who seeks an abortion for her reasons to make sure legal requirements are fulfilled; therefore, women may freely have abortions, which means that abortions based on abnormalities are possible. So, if a doctor does not inform a patient of the possibility of a congenital abnormality, it may raise the problem of 'wrongful birth'. Concerning congenital rubella syndrome, district courts decided for the plaintiff parents in part. But these may differ from each other concerning economic damages. In two cases where the plaintiff only claimed compensation for emotional distress and attorney's fees, the court affirmed the claim without mentioning economic damage (945 Hanreijihou 65 (Tokyo Dist. Ct., 18 September 1979), 1100 Hanreijihou89 (Tokyo Dist. Ct., 22 July 1983)). In two other cases, plaintiffs claimed not ONLY emotional distress but also medical and care fees, but the courts only affirmed the claim for emotional distress and rejected the latter claim. The reasoning of one court was that there was no legal causation between negligence of the defendant doctor and such economic damage; there was no provision for congenital defect in the (then) Eugenics Protection Act, and the decision to give birth to the child or not was a highly moral one (1468 Hanreijihou 116 (Tokyo Dist. Ct., 8 July 1992)). The reasoning of another court was that abortion based on the foetus' abnormality was impossible after its birth, and it was not appropriate for a court to compare the amount of loss that was incurred when the child was born alive and the amount that would have been incurred had the foetus been aborted (809 Hanreitaimuzu 189 (Maebashi Dist. Ct., 15 December 1992)). Those two courts did affirm compensation for emotional distress based on the right to know and prepare for the birth of a baby with a disorder.

On the other hand, concerning Down Syndrome, one district court decided against the plaintiff parents and rejected the claim of compensation for emotional distress (1628 Hanreijihou 71 (Kyoto Dist. Ct., 24 January 1997)). It said that:

(1) even if amniocentesis had been done the result would have come back only after the lawful period (twenty-two weeks of gestation), so the plaintiff could not choose whether to bear or abort the child; and
(2) doctors did not have a duty to tell the 39-year-old woman about amniocentesis because there was no way to compare the severity of her emotional shock upon being told during pregnancy that the foetus had abnormalities and her shock upon learning of these abnormalities after childbirth.

It may be worth adding that a professional committee under MHLW issued an opinion paper on maternal serum tests in 1999, in which it said that doctors do not need to tell a pregnant woman about the test and that if a pregnant woman asks, doctors should tell her the nature and limits of the test and that a disability does not necessarily become a burden to the baby and to his/her family.[121]

121. www1.mhlw.go.jp/houdou/1107/h0721-1_18.html.

In 2013, two types of diagnosis attracted interest; one is MaterniT21™ PLUS non-Invasive Prenatal Test (hereinafter NIPT) conducted by Sequenom, an American company, and another is a combination of (traditional) echo test and maternal serum screening test.

NIPT is done in ninety-two hospitals certified by the Japanese Association of Medical Sciences (JAMS) as clinical research with genetic counselling as of July 2018.[122] It is reported that in three and a half years, 37,506 women have taken the test, and the results are: diagnosed as positive 763, affirmed as having chromosomal abnormality by amniocentesis 508; and 476 (94%) women chose abortion, 13 chose the continuance of pregnancy and 19 (natural) deaths of infants.[123] According to another press, 27,696 pregnant women underwent NIPT altogether from its introduction in April 2013 to December 2015 in which 469 of them (1.7%) were tested positive for one of the chromosomal abnormalities, Trisomy 13, 18 or 21. When the amniocentesis was undertaken to confirm the diagnosis, 35 individuals were found to have foetuses with no abnormalities, while 73 went on to have either miscarriages or stillbirths. There are also cases that are unaccounted for. Among the remaining confirmed 346 cases, 334 women chose termination. Meanwhile, 12 women opted to continue their pregnancies.[124]

In 2016, it was also reported that a few clinics offered NIPT/D without the certification of JAMS, for which the Japan Society of Obstetrics and Gynaecology disciplined three doctors (two warnings, one reprimand). The clinics advertised on their website that they sent samples to Genesis Genetics, a United Kingdom laboratory. This incident was enough to worry the Society. It declared the end of the clinical research stage in March 2018 saying it had enough evidence on the importance of genetic counselling and changed its guidelines such that general institutions certified by the Japan Association of Medical Sciences could also perform NIPT.[125] The Society also tried to loosen the requirement to perform NIPT so that even clinics were able to get certification in order to guarantee access to pregnant women, and among them was the non-requirement of the clinical genetic specialist certification to offer genetic counselling and involvement of full-time paediatrician if certain conditions were met.[126] However, it drew criticism from the Japan Society of Human Genetics and the Japan Pediatric Society when the draft revision guidelines were made public. The main argument of the Japan Pediatric Society was as follows. They were aware that the proliferation of NIPT might bring about serious situations such as trying to deny the existence of children with chromosomal diseases even though they acknowledged that the rights and self-determination of pregnant women and her family were to be respected. They believed that pregnant women and their families needed qualified genetic counselling and information on the real lives of children with chromosomal diseases and their families. However, it

122. http://jams.med.or.jp/rinshobukai_ghs/facilities.html.
123. The Asahi Shimbun, December/17/2016.
124. '96.5% of pregnant women who found abnormalities in new prenatal test aborted' 25 Apr. 2016, at https://mainichi.jp/english/articles/20160425/p2a/00m/0na/025000c.
125. Norikazu Chiba 'Japan ob-gyn society considering looser requirements for new prenatal genetic test' The Mainichi, 15 May 2018 at https://mainichi.jp/english/articles/20180515/p2a/00m/0na/005000c.
126. http://www.jsog.or.jp/uploads/files/news/NIPT_shishin_20190622.pdf.

would deprive pregnant women and their families of their opportunity to think about other options and also the society of living together with people with chromosomal diseases if the involvements of paediatricians were inadequate.[127] The Japan Society of Human Genetics also stressed the importance of genetic counselling and collaboration of many disciplines such as obstetrics and gynaecology, paediatrics, clinical genetics for pregnant women, foetuses and their families.[128] As the discussion between stakeholders seemed to be inadequate, the MHLW took this matter to its ambit and requested the Japan Society of Obstetrics and Gynaecology to deal with the expansion of NIPT after necessary discussions by the consultation committee on NIPT set up by the state on 21 June 2019.[129] This committee published its final report in May 2021,[130] proposing a committee will be held under the JAMS.

The combination of (traditional) echo test and maternal serum screening test is also provided as clinical research in six large hospitals. On the other hand, echo test is done regularly in clinics, which eventually may provide test result of foetus abnormality by the nuchal translucency.

§2. Sterilization

88. Sterilization was provided for in the National Eugenics Act (1940) (and its successor Eugenics Protection Act (1948), described below). As the title itself indicates, these acts aimed to prevent the reproduction of those who had 'bad' genes and to improve the nature of the nation (Article 1). The Act provided that those who had a hereditary mental disease, hereditary mental retardation, severe hereditary personality disorder, severe hereditary physical illness or highly hereditary malformation, or who had such relatives within the fourth degree, *might* be sterilized (Article 3). It also provided that directors of mental hospitals (provided in the above Mental Hospitals Act) or local public health officers who cared for those who had such conditions might request the (then) district officer to sterilize such people (with the consent of the person concerned in principle (Article 5), although in special cases, consent was not needed (Article 6)). Compulsory sterilization was possible and, indeed, was performed.

After WWII, its successor Eugenics Protection Act expanded the conditions to instances in which the person concerned or his/her spouse had leprosy[131] which might be transmitted to children, or during pregnancy or delivery might pose a risk to the woman. Doctors might perform sterilization with the consent of the person

127. http://www.jpeds.or.jp/modules/guidelines/index.php?content_id=106.
128. https://jshg.jp/wp-content/uploads/2019/03/1e29e36e99990dfa47972e61c402c78f.pdf.
129. http://www.jsog.or.jp/uploads/files/news/NIPT_kourousho.pdf.
130. https://www.mhlw.go.jp/content/000783387.pdf.
131. Leprosy patients were detained in special institutions by the Leprosy Prevention Act, and it is reported that patients underwent (compulsory) sterilization in such institutions before enactment of the Eugenics Protection Act. It is also reported that compulsory sterilizations were continued after this enactment, until recently. Leprosy is not a hereditary disease, and this was known by the time of enactment of the Eugenics Protection Act. Sterilization based on leprosy was aimed to exclude leprosy patients from society, so it might be said that this was based on eugenics in a broad sense.

concerned, except when he/she was a minor or had a mental disease or mental retardation (Article 3).[132] The doctor had to petition the prefectural eugenics protection committee for sterilization if he/she diagnosed a hereditary disease, malformation or retardation in a patient[133] or if he/she thought it would be in the public interest (Article 4). Moreover, the doctor might request permission to sterilize if he/she diagnosed other mental diseases and if a caregiver of the patient gave consent (Article 12). Sterilization, for other reasons, was prohibited (Article 28).[134] The victims of the forced sterilization filed lawsuits in 2018, insisting that the Eugenics Protection Act was unconstitutional and the sterilization was illegal,[135] but district courts rejected them on the ground of extinctive prescription.

The Leprosy Prevention Act was abolished in 1996. When the Eugenics Protection Act was amended in 1997 (and renamed the Maternity Protection Act), provisions on sterilization were practically deleted. There remains only one section; sterilization with the consent of the person concerned (and of his/her spouse, if any) is lawful, except in the case of a minor (Article 3).

§3. Assisted Reproductive Technology

I. Regulations on ART

A. *Introduction*

89. There were no statutes or rules concerning procedures for ART in Japan until 2020 as we shall introduce and discuss later. Until then, as cases of post-mortem insemination and surrogacy drew public attention, governmental advisory bodies filed reports suggesting the need for regulation. Before we look into the advisory reports, let us look at the history of ART in Japan. It was in August 1949 that the first child conceived through Artificial Insemination by Donor (AID) was born at Keio University. Five years after Louise Brown was born in the United Kingdom, the first child conceived by in vitro fertilization (IVF) was born at Tohoku University in March 1983. The Japan Society of Obstetrics and Gynaecology issued many sets of statements on ART and the research use of embryos and gametes.

The Society issued its 'Statement on IVF and Embryo Transfer' soon after the first child conceived by IVF was born in 1983. It was revised in 2006 and 2014, but the core of the statement is unchanged. It states that IVF-ET is a medical procedure

132. This exception was understood as a prohibition of sterilization of such people, that is, such people were treated as incompetent concerning sterilization.
133. 'Hereditary mental disease' includes schizophrenia, manic-depressive psychosis and epilepsy, and 'hereditary physical disease' includes Huntington's disease, ataxia, colour blindness, hereditary deafness and haemophilia (provided in the schedule).
134. Thus, a doctor who performed sex reassignment surgery on a patient with gender-identity-disorder was judged as guilty of this prohibition (23 Koukeishuu 759 (Tokyo App. Ct., 11 Nov. 1970)).
135. Committee on the Elimination of Discrimination against Women of the United Nations published a report https://tbinternet.ohchr.org/_layouts/treatybodyexternal/Download.aspx?symbolno=CEDAW%2fC%2fJPN%2fCO%2f7-8&Lang=en >, and discussed the issue in paras 24 and 25.

used to treat infertile couples,[136] so it should be carried out with recognition of its ethical, legal and social implications and also its safety and effectiveness. It must be carried out by an experienced doctor on the condition that the chances for the couple to conceive without IVF-ET are none or extremely low, and that the couple gives informed consent and is married. No genetic manipulation is to be performed. The Society is against embryo donation[137] and post-mortem insemination. Also, it advises Society members to destroy cryopreserved sperm when the donor dies (Statement in 2007). It issued a 'Statement against Surrogacy' in April 2003 after surrogacy cases involving Japanese couples performed in the US and in Japan were reported. It is quite interesting that the Society issues statements after events involving ART are reported, but the practice of AID had not been the subject of a statement for a long time. The Society finally issued a 'Statement on AID' in 1997 which was revised in 2006 and 2015. The title of the statement was changed to 'Statement on Artificial Insemination using Donated Sperm' to make clear what it deals with. It states that AID is a medical procedure used to treat infertile couples, so it should be carried out with recognition for its ethical, legal and social implications. It must be carried out on the condition that the couple cannot conceive without this technology or that without this technology the mother or the baby would be in danger, that the couple gives informed consent and is married.[138] The privacy of the couple and the prospective child is to be protected. The sperm donor is to be anonymous to protect his privacy, but his records must be kept by the doctor who performed the procedure. The donor must be in good health physically and mentally, with no known infectious or genetic disease. AID must be carried out using cryopreserved sperm to avoid the danger of infectious disease. The number of children born with the same donor's sperm is limited to ten. The donation of sperms should not be carried out for profit purposes. All procedures using artificial insemination technology must be registered and reported to the Society now.[139] There's also a statement on the cryopreservation of unfertilized eggs, embryos (fertilized eggs) and ovarian tissues for medical indication. It deals with the preservation of eggs for people suffering from diseases such as malignant tumour who may have a chance to become infertile in the course of treatment. The preservation of eggs is performed as a medical procedure, so the attending physician and another physician who is in charge of reproduction give details of the procedure such as risks and benefits and also the current uncertainties and details of ART using cryopreserved eggs. In the case of a minor patient who is considered to have enough understanding, the informed consent of both legal representatives (usually parents) and the patient must be obtained.

136. The Society deleted the word 'married' in 2017 because it's difficult for doctors to ask the disclosure of privacy from patients, so it still means that those techniques are to be used for heterosexual couples.
137. The reason is as follows. The first is that the welfare of the prospective child should be paramount, and secondly, it may lead to complication of the parent-child relationship.
138. The Society requires 'marriage' for AID, because it considers the welfare of the child. As we will see, there are legal cases on filiation using donated sperms, so it has worry that the child-to-be-born has a chance to be rejected by the prospective father (husband). In the procedure to perform this technique, the couple must affirm in the informed consent form to accept the prospective child as their legitimate child.
139. Those statements are on http://www.jsog.or.jp/modules/statement/index.php?content_id=3.

However, these strict society statements are, sometimes, disregarded by doctors who have strong convictions to assist infertile couples. They may be ousted from the Society as a result, but they are not subject to any criminal or administrative sanctions, and they are also able to re-enter the society after a while.

There have been moves toward legislation. A special committee on ART under the MHW published a report on the proper regulation of ART in 2000. The report raises six areas of concern:

(1) the welfare of a child born via the technology;
(2) the problem of treating people only as a means of procreation;
(3) security;
(4) the problem of eugenics;
(5) the problem of commercialism; and
(6) respect for human dignity.

As a result, it was suggested that surrogacy be banned. Following this report, a committee on ART under the MHLW published a report establishing grounds for regulations of ART in April 2003. Surrogacy is banned according to this report as well. AID and IVF using donor eggs and surplus fertilized eggs are permitted according to this report, but it is suggested that frozen sperm be destroyed after the donor's death. Following the report on the suggestion of proper regulation of ART, the Legislative Council of the Ministry of Justice issued an interim report in July 2003 on the legal nature of the parent-child relationship concerning children born via ART. According to this interim report, the legal mother is the one who gives birth to the child, and the child born via AID is the child of the husband if the AID was performed with the husband's consent. The new act enacted in 2020 is called the 'Act on the Use and Regulation of Assisted Reproductive Technologies (ART) and on the Special Provisions of the Civil Code regarding the Parentage of Resultant Children' (hereinafter 'the Act on ART 2020') and is virtually the same as the interim report.

II. Parent-Child Relationship

A. *Introduction*

90. The parent-child relationship becomes complicated when ART is involved in begetting children. The following section discusses the establishment of paternity in cases of AID and post-mortem insemination and the establishment of maternity in cases of surrogacy.

B. *Who Is the Child's Father in AID Cases?*

91. Relevant provisions of the Civil Code of Japan in establishing paternity are as follows. Section 772(1) provides that a child born during a marriage is presumed to be the child of the husband. However, §774 provides that the husband has a right to deny the legitimacy of the child. Also, §776 provides that the husband loses his right to deny the legitimacy of the child if he accepted the child as legitimate.

There are some cases on the establishment of paternity via AID. One was a custody case after divorce where the Tokyo Appellate Court ruled that when AID is performed with the consent of the husband, the child born via the procedure is the child of the marriage, and the wife cannot claim denial of paternity (51-3 Kateisaibangeppou 165 (Tokyo App. Ct., 16 September 1998)). Another case was a denial of paternity and legitimacy of the child by the husband when the father did not give consent to the AID procedure (51-9 Kateisaibangeppou 71 (Osaka Dist. Ct., 18 December 1998)).

92. In the latter Osaka District Court case, the court held that the husband might deny the paternity of the child.

The facts of the case are as follows: X (wife) and Y (husband, plaintiff) were married in 1992. They wanted a child, but as they could not bear a child naturally, they went to a fertility clinic to receive treatment in 1993. They tried artificial insemination, fertilized egg implantation, and frozen fertilized egg implantation five times in total. X became pregnant once and thereafter miscarried, and no pregnancy resulted from the other four times. In May 1995, X went to another clinic to try AID, became pregnant, and gave birth to a child (defendant) on 27 January 1996. Y claimed that X had extramarital affairs, and the defendant was not his child. Also, he claimed that he did not agree to use donor sperm. X, as a person who has parental responsibility for the defendant, counterclaimed that Y agreed to the use of donor sperm, and even if this were not the case, Y had accepted the defendant as his child by naming the child and turning in the birth certificate form to the registry. X tried to invoke §776 to deny Y's right under §774.

The court ruled that no evidence had been produced to convince the court to conclude that the plaintiff agreed to the use of donor sperm. Although both husband and wife were getting old and it was their last chance to conceive a child around 1996, that does not necessarily lead to the conclusion that the plaintiff agreed comprehensively to the use of donor sperm. Also, X's claims that their relationship was in turmoil from 1994 and that it was unimportant for the plaintiff whose sperms were used, were not convincing either. If the marriage was in turmoil, then the plaintiff had no reason to want to assume responsibility for a child conceived using unknown donor's sperm.

As to the approval of legitimacy claim, the court was not convinced that the plaintiff accepted the child as legitimate even though there was evidence that the plaintiff named the child, turned in the birth certificate form to the registry, and even tried to borrow money for an operation to correct the child's cleft palate. Judgment was for the plaintiff, and paternity was denied.

Recently, it was decided by the Supreme Court that a gender dysphoria person (hereinafter referred to as GD), who changed sex from female to male in the family register and was married to a female wife and begot a child through AID is presumed to be the father of the child and is to be registered as the legal father of the child (Sup. Ct., 10 December 2013).[140] There is a special statute concerning the change of registration of the sex for the GDs who meet the requirement of the statute. The Female to Male (FtM) person at bar met the requirement and, thereafter, was treated as male. So, he was able to get married to his wife. However, he could not beget a child through sexual intercourse, so the couple thought of having a child with AID. The reasoning of the Supreme Court is as follows: even though it is not possible for the FtM husband to beget a child through sexual intercourse with his wife, it is not fair to deny the main effect of marriage (to have children and establish paternity) when he is allowed to marry, just because he cannot have a child naturally. The decision can be appreciated as protecting family privacy and also treating the sexual minority equally under the Constitution. (*See* how the case at bar is treated, compared with the two infertile married couple's AID cases introduced above.)

C. Who Is the Child's Father in Post-mortem Insemination Cases?

93. As the Civil Code was enacted in 1898, it did not envision cases of post-mortem insemination and the establishment of paternity, so there is no particular article on these matters. Therefore, when children born via post-mortem insemination filed lawsuits to acknowledge the legal father-child relationship, the courts of Japan and academics were divided on this issue. There are two reported cases (one involving a de facto marriage) and one unpublished case, but the most important is undoubtedly the case with a published Supreme Court ruling.

94. A mother, on behalf of the child, filed a suit against the public prosecutor to acknowledge the paternity of the child conceived with the dead husband's cryopreserved sperm under §787 of the Civil Code. Here, it should be noted that the public prosecutor, as a representative of the public good, is the defendant in acknowledgement cases after the death of a husband.

95. The Matsuyama District Court, on 12 November 2003, held that the legal relationship between the father and the child must be examined in light of social norms and attitudes considering the following factors: ensuring the child's well-being, harmony with the order of family law, similarity between the ART concerned and the natural course of reproduction, and whether the ART concerned is socially accepted. Each case should be determined considering its specific circumstances.

In this case, the court hesitated to acknowledge the deceased father as the legal father of the child conceived with the preserved sperm after his death. The case was dismissed, and the plaintiff appealed to the Takamatsu Appellate Court.

96. The Takamatsu Appellate Court, on 16 July 2004, held that when a child is conceived through artificial insemination, in order to approve the claims of acknowledgement, it is only required that the child and the father have a biological parent-child relationship and that the father agreed to that particular conception,

140. http://www.courts.go.jp/search/jhsp0030?hanreiid=83810&hanreiKbn=02.

except in cases when approval of acknowledgement is not justified under the particular circumstances of the case. In this case, the appellant child and the sperm donor (the deceased husband) had a biological parent-child relationship, and the evidence was enough to convince the court that the deceased husband agreed to the use of his sperm after his death for his wife to conceive their child, and there were no special circumstances to assume that the acknowledgement was unjustified.

Judgment was reversed, and the claims of the appellant were approved. The public prosecutor then appealed to the Supreme Court.

97. The Supreme Court, on 4 September 2006 (60-7 Minshu 2563), held that civil law does not presuppose a parent-child relationship between the deceased father and the child conceived after the father's death using his cryopreserved sperm. That is to say, the relationship between the deceased father and the child conceived after his death does not give rise to the fundamental legal relationship prescribed by the civil law, such as custody, support and inheritance. So, the establishment of the legal relationship between them has to be resolved considering many factors such as the bioethics of the ART using the deceased person's sperm, the welfare of the child born via the technology, the consciousness of the people who will have a parental or familial relationship with the child, and the consciousness of society as a whole. The court ruled that because so many factors need to be taken into account, this is a problem that should be resolved by the legislature. As no pertinent law was in existence, the establishment of paternity between the father and child was denied.

98. As we have seen, the Supreme Court denied the establishment of paternity. In fact, the Takamatsu Appellate Court was the only court that approved the legal relationship between the father and the child. The Supreme Court confirmed that the deceased father's approval when he was alive has nothing to do with the establishment of paternity, and the relationship between the deceased father and the child conceived after his death does not give rise to the fundamental legal relationship.

The first point is a very interesting one. It is argued that the decision to bear children after one's death is different from the self-determination which is usually protected by law because the interests of the children-to-be-born have to be taken into account and the legal parent-child relationship is established according to the public order. As to the second point, the deceased father does not have any room to have parental rights, and the child will not receive care, nurture and support from him and will not inherit his estate. Thus, this relationship does not give rise to the fundamental legal parent-child relationship. As the court does not have active law-making powers, it is up to the legislature to decide whether paternity would be established and on what grounds.

D. Who Is the Child's Mother in Cases Involving Donated Eggs and a Surrogate/Host Mother?

99. There are a few cases on surrogacy in Japan, that is, one in which a de facto married couple used donated eggs (1919 Hanreijihou 107 (Osaka App. Ct., 23 May

2005), *aff'd*, Sup. Ct., 24 November 2005 (not reported)), and a famous reported Supreme Court case about a television personality couple who used fertilized eggs that had a genetic relationship to them (Tokyo App. Ct., 29 September 2006 granted the claim, but *rev'd*, 61-2 Minshu 619 (Sup. Ct., 23 March 2007)). In both cases, the children were born via surrogate mothers in the US and were given birth certificates with the intending mothers' names on them. Both cases reached the Supreme Court, and both of the intending mothers lost the legal battle to win maternity status. There is only one article on determining the child's mother (Civil Code §779),[141] and according to that article, the mother may acknowledge the child out of wedlock. It was then argued whether the acknowledgement of the mother is needed to establish maternity and it was decided by the Supreme Court in 1962 that in order to establish a relationship between a mother and a child out of wedlock, the mother's acknowledgement is not necessary, in principle, but the fact that delivery naturally leads to the establishment of maternity (16-7 Minshu 1247 (Sup. Ct., 27 April 1962)). The reason for this decision is that maternity is obvious from the delivery and the child's status is stable when the person giving birth becomes the legal mother. It is the same with regard to a child born to a married couple, where the person giving birth to the child is the legal mother. This is considered as the fundamental principle of law and order that cannot be changed by the intention of persons involved, so it naturally applies to surrogacy cases as well. That is why the Supreme Court rejected the Tokyo Appellate Court's ruling, which had established the mother-child relationship between the intending mother and children born from the surrogate mother. The Supreme Court ruled that the birth certificate issued by the foreign country is not acceptable because it violates the basic principle and/or the fundamentals of law and order in Japan. Following this famous surrogacy case, the Society of Obstetrics and Gynaecology asked the government to enact a law on ART, and the Minister of HLW and the Minister of Justice referred this to the Science Council of Japan. The advisory report, issued in April 2008,[142] suggested that surrogacy be regulated by law and be banned, in principle, and that surrogacy with a commercial purpose be banned by criminal law. However, it is also suggested that there should be an exception to allow clinical trials of surrogacy under strict control in cases of absolute (medical) indication. This suggestion for allowing an exception drew much criticism. As for the parent-child relationship, it was suggested that the surrogate mother become the legal mother, and the intending couple establishes a parent-child relationship by adoption.

141. Article 787 of the Civil Code (filing a lawsuit for acknowledgement of the child): 'A child … or his/her legal representative has a right to file a lawsuit for acknowledgement. However, it is subjected to 3 years limitation after the death of the father.'
142. www.scj.go.jp/ja/info/kohyo/pdf/kohyo-20-t56-1.pdf.

E. The Act on ART 2020[143]

100. This act was promulgated on 11 December 2020. It is the first law to address the issue on ART, but it is limited in scope and contains only two articles on the ascertainment of parentage of children that are of little meaning.

This act consists of three chapters and supplementary provisions. Chapter one consists of two articles. Article 1 is about the purpose of this act, i.e., 'to clarify the fundamental principles on the use of ART, to stipulate the responsibilities of healthcare providers and the state, and also the measures to be taken by the state, and to make amendments to the civil code about the parent-child relationship when ART using third party's sperm and/or ova are performed', and Article 2 provides the definition of ART.

Chapter two (Articles 3 to 8) is about the use of ART. Article 4 stipulates the responsibility of the state and Article 5 the responsibility of the healthcare providers. Articles 6 to 8 stipulate the state's responsibility in striving to disseminate the information about ART, and to construct the counselling system and the legal system, respectively. Article 3 is on the fundamental principles which lacks concrete substance. Article 3(1) is on the protection of the health of women who are to be pregnant and to give birth using ART. It also makes sure that ART is used as treatments for infertility only. Article 3(2) is on obtaining the informed consent of each party involved. Article 3(3) is on securing the safety in obtaining and storing the sperm and ova for ART. Article 3(4) provides that, 'due regard is to be paid for children born by ART to be born and grow up healthy, both physically and mentally'. It is the most controversial article and drew much criticism from the disability groups as the phrase, 'to be born healthy … both physically and mentally' raises the spectre of eugenics in the hearts and minds of people with disability. Article 3 should have stipulated important principles such as the supremacy of the child's best interests and the exclusion of practices based on eugenics.

The act should also have given children born as a result of ART the right to access information about the donor as it is of vital importance to guarantee the fulfilment of the natural, personal interest of knowing one's biological heritage and establishing the identity of oneself. The act also does not cover other issues such as the regulations on commercial procurement of eggs and sperm and surrogacy services. It is sad to say that all those years of discussions among experts on law, social sciences, and medicine, among others before and after the report of a committee on ART under the MHLW in 2003 are not reflected at all. Also, it does not say anything about who is eligible or ineligible to use ART in this act's scheme, so we must address the issues on the use of the technique by sexual minorities while examining the laws and experiences of other jurisdictions.

---

143. *See*, Yuko Nagamizu:

> In Search of an Appropriate Policy on Regulating Assisted Reproductive Technologies and Ascertaining the Parentage of Children Born as a Result of ART: Critical Examination of 'the Act on ART 2020' in Japan, 35 Momoyama Hougaku (Law Review) 1-55 (English summary (pp 43-55) follows the Japanese article) (https://www.jstage.jst.go.jp/article/momoyamahougaku/35/0/35_1/_article/-char/ja/), for details. (English summary follows the Japanese article) (in print), for details.

Chapter three is on the ascertainment of parentage of children born as a result of ART. Article 9 is on the mother-child relationship and it stipulates that, 'a woman who is pregnant and gives birth using a donated egg (including an embryo derived from the egg) is the child's mother'. This only reflects the current state of law in Japan as we saw earlier, and the act merely elucidates it. Article 10 is on the father-child relationship and it stipulates that, 'a husband who gives consent to his wife giving birth with a donated sperm (including an embryo derived from the sperm) will be unable to deny the legitimacy of the child, despite the Article 774 of the civil law'.[144] This too is merely a reflection of the current state of case law in Japan as discussed earlier, but the legislatures made it clear to ensure the stability of paternity.

The part on the amendment to the civil law (Chapter 3 of the act) will come into effect on 11 December 2021 and apply to children born from that day on. Also, according to the supplementary provision Article 3, the act is scheduled to be amended over the following two years in order to secure the appropriate use of ART, so the members of the Houses will continue to address issues concerning the appropriate governance of ART, regulations on the donation of sperm, ova, and embryos and/or the regulations on the procurement/transaction of them, and the system of storage, management and disclosure of personal information of donors, recipients and children born with ART. It also stipulates that the provisions on the ascertainment of parentage may be amended to further the stability of parent-child relationship born as a result of ART, based on the amendments to the new regulations of ART, if necessary.

§4. Genetic Diagnosis, Insurance and Gene Therapy

I. Genetic Diagnosis and Insurance

101. In socialized health insurance, genetic diagnoses of muscular dystrophy and some types of cancer, and associated genetic counselling are approved. On the other hand, 'Direct to Consumer' genetic tests are not regulated, so available by mail order or through the website.

The health insurance system is run under the very strict control of the government, so discrimination on the results of genetic testing in health insurance has not occurred,[145] but with regard to life insurance, one case may be of interest, though strictly speaking this is not a genetic discrimination case.

102. Plaintiff had gotten treatment for a problem in his legs and had made a contract with the defendant insurance company in 1989 which read that the company should pay 'when the insured becomes highly disabled because of injury or disease

144. Article 774 of the civil law gives a husband the right to deny paternity if he finds out that the child is not biologically connected with him, but he has to file a lawsuit within one year after the child is born (Art. 777 of the civil law).

145. *See* Japanese national report in 'Genetic Testing and the Governance of Risk in the Contemporary Economy' (Springer, 2020).

which occurred after the start of liable term, including when new injury or disease is added to ones before the term'. In 1992, the plaintiff was officially classified as highly disabled, and in 1995 the plaintiff had a galactosylceramidase activation test and was diagnosed as having Krabbe disease. Before and after this diagnosis, the defendant insurance company had paid for the plaintiff's hospitalization. The plaintiff claimed disability insurance, but the defendant refused on the ground that the plaintiff had already had a disability before the liable term. The plaintiff argued in court that the defendant's refusal was against the public order because he had a right to have an advanced medical test, but the denial was based on the diagnosis of Krabbe disease, which he had a right to know. He also insisted that claims on all genetic diseases would be refused even if he became ill after the contract went into effect.

The district court (1198 Kinyuushoujihanrei 55 (Kobe Dist. Ct., 18 June 2003)) denied the plaintiff's claim based on the term in the above contract, that is, the insurer has to pay only when the disease occurs after the contract had gone into effect. It denied the plaintiff's argument on nature and the need for protection of genetic information because, in this case, genetic information was not provided from the insured to the insurer. The appellate court (1198 Kinyuushoujihanrei 48 (Osaka App. Ct., 27 May 2004)) partially granted the plaintiff's claim and demanded that the defendant pay JPY 10 million on the ground of estoppel; the insured had made several claims to the regional branch, but the head of the branch had explained that it would be better not to claim at that time and had advised the plaintiff to claim later when the situation became worse. The court also stated as obiter dicta that this case had the same root that the problem of genetic information had, but that genetic information may not be excluded from evidence because there was no special statutory regulation.

II. Gene Therapy and Genome Editing

103. Some kinds of gene therapy have been provided in Japan as clinical research under administrative guidelines.[146] The first gene therapy was provided to a minor patient with Adenosine Deaminase deficiency in 1995. But adverse incidents in the US and France hindered such practices elsewhere, and, as of 2006, only twenty-one types of gene therapies have been performed in Japan.[147] Concerning genome editing technique, the bioethics subcommittee under the Council for Science, Technology and Innovation is now discussing the application of genome editing on human fertilized eggs, which issued an interim report on 13 December 2016 which permits fundamental research if the research is approved by a research ethics committee.

146. At first, the MHW and the MEXT respectively had issued their own guidelines (MHW guidelines were for non-university hospitals and those of the MEXT were for university hospitals). But the two issued a set of guidelines jointly in 2002. *See* www.mext.go.jp/a_menu/shinkou/seimei/gene/04122801.htm.

147. www.nihart.go.jp/cgtp/cgtp/sec1/gt_prtcl/prtcl-e.html.

In July 2022, MHLW approved teserpaturev (G47Δ; Delytact^{R}) for malignant glioma, which consists of Herpes simplex virus recombinant DNA which can replicate in glioma cells.[148]

§5. Organ Transplantation

I. Brief History of Organ Transplantation and Its Regulation

104. In Japan, the first corneal transplant was done in 1949 at Iwate Medical University (a private university) by a professor. Later, the professor established an eye bank and did a transplant using a cornea from the eye bank in 1957. But there was a fear that removal of corneas from a cadaver might constitute 'destruction of cadaver' as described in the Criminal Code (Article 190). So, the legislature enacted the Corneal Transplant Act in 1958 to make it lawful to remove corneas from a cadaver if there was written authorization of surviving relative(s).

In 1969, this was succeeded by the Corneal and Renal Transplant Act. The requirement was the same as in the Corneal Transplant Act, that is, authorization of surviving relative(s). Neither the person's consent nor refusal appeared as a condition in the text, and whether surviving relative(s) may authorize removal against the person's refusal during his/her lifetime was unclear.[149]

II. Heart Transplantation and Brain Death

105. In 1968, soon after Dr Christian Barnard performed the first heart transplant in South Africa, Professor Wada at Sapporo Medical School (a municipal university) performed a heart transplant. The recipient died less than three months later, and after the transplant, it was reported that he had a problem only in the mitral valve (Professor Wada said that the patient had problems in multiple valves and he could not treat him by artificial valve replacement). Also, Chiro it was reported that the treatment received by the donor patient had been problematic. Therefore, this transplant was criticized on the basis that the selection of the recipient was not proper and that there was room for life-saving of the donor. This put the brakes on transplantation, especially from brain-dead cadavers. After this, no heart transplants were performed in Japan for thirty years.

106. In the 1980s and 1990s, there were many debates on organ transplantation, especially on brain death and the 'right to self-determination' of the deceased. Two drafts were proposed in the parliament, both based on 'self-determination' of the deceased. One provided brain death as human death (regardless of transplant) and

---

148. https://www.onclive.com/view/oncolytic-virus-teserpaturev-approved-in-japan-for-malignant-glioma.

149. A criminal law professor asserted that to permit removal on relatives' consent when the person concerned had opposed the idea is unconstitutional. Fumio Kanazawa, *Zouki Ishoku to Shoudaku*, 8 Hiroshima Hougaku 1 (1984).

the other did not allow brain death as a death criterion but permitted removal of an organ. These two approaches were merged and became law in 1997. The Act permitted the removal of an organ (heart, lung, liver, kidney, pancreas and small intestine) and eyeball (Article 5)). The fundamental principles of this Act were:

(1) respect for the wishes of the donor;
(2) voluntary nature of the donation;
(3) appropriate transplantation for the benefit of persons in need of transplant;
(4) fair allocation of chances for organ transplantation (Article 2. They were not changed by the 2009 amendment).

The requirements for organ removal were:

(1) the deceased person's written expression of intention;[150] and
(2) no refusal of surviving relative(s) (if any) to (a) organ donation, and (b) application of brain death diagnosis (Article 6).

There was no definition of relative(s) in the Act, but guidelines issued by the MHLW defined that doctors should receive consent from a spouse, children, father and mother, grandson, grandfather and grandmother, and other relatives who lived with the deceased, and that relatives' opinions should be collected by the chief mourner (before WWII, 'Koshu' often became the chief mourner, but now the surviving spouse generally becomes the chief mourner). In practice, transplant team (doctors, nurses and coordinators) not only confirmed that there was no refusal but also sought positive consent from surviving relative(s). So both the person concerned and surviving relative(s) had the right to (a) and (b). If either of the two would not consent to (a) or (b), no organ removal should be done. But schedule 4 provided that kidneys and eyeballs may be removed from a donor whose heart had ceased beating (i.e., the donor is defined as dead by traditional criteria) where there is surviving relatives' written consent, which was permitted in the 1969 Act.

150. In the Act, there is no provision on the competency to become a donor, but of course a donor must have the ability of understanding and decision-making on organ donation. Guidelines issued by the MHLW provide that potential donors should be 15 years old or more following the requirement of making a will in the Civil Code. The Act provides that a donor is the deceased person and that only the donor may make an organ donation, which means that organ donation by the surviving family members is not allowed. Therefore transplantation to a child recipient cannot be provided in Japan. This is a big problem, especially in children with congenital heart defects. They cannot receive transplants in Japan, so they have to go overseas, which requires much money and time. In the Diet, amendment of the Act has been discussed (there are two amendments proposed; one permits organ donation by family members, and another permits organ donation by a donor who is 12 years old or more). As stated below, 2009 amendment permits organ donation with surviving relatives' authorization, so organ transplant to a child became lawful.

107. This Act became effective in October 1997, but the first transplant from a brain-dead donor occurred in February 1999. Since then, there have been 76 brain-dead transplants (at the end of 2008), in which 60 hearts, 53 lungs, 58 livers, 54 pancreases and 133 kidneys have been transplanted, whereas 1,493 kidneys have been transplanted from non-heart-beating cadavers. This was far from the necessary number.

III. Current Statute

108. The Diet passed an amendment of the Act in 2009, and this became effective in July 2010. It permits organ removal not only with the donor's expressed will but also with surviving relatives' will. This means that both the deceased and surviving family members may donate organs. The first donation with relatives' authorization occurred on 9 August. News coverage reports that the deceased expressed his wish of organ donation to his family, and the family members expressed the will of donation according to his wish. There were four donations with relatives' authorization in one month, whereas there was one donation with donor's authorization. It was estimated that the number of organ donation would be about eighty per year, which meant ten times before the amendment. In 2020, there were 68 donations from brain-dead donors and there were 54 heart transplants, 58 lung transplant, 58 liver transplants, 5 liver-kidney transplants, 4 pancreas transplants, 24 pancreas-kidney transplants, 112 kidney transplants and 3 small intestine transplants.[151]

109. Once removed, the organ may not be used for any purpose other than transplantation (it should be disposed of by cremation as provided in the regulations (Article 9)), that is, if the organ is not transplantable, it may not be used for research, even if the deceased gave consent to such a use.

110. The Act does not regulate living donation (except organ sales as stated below). But this does not mean that living donation is not common in Japan. In 2019, 1,827 kidneys and 307 livers were transplanted from living donors.[152] Further, the number of living liver transplants to adults (18 years and more, and 50s is the most) is increasing, which means the larger part of the liver (right lobe) is removed and transplanted.[153] In 2003, a donor died from liver failure. The Japanese Liver Transplantation Society does follow-up investigations of the health-related problems of living donors.[154] A ban on offering and receiving remuneration is applied to the transfer of transplantable material from both a deceased donor and a living donor. There are two cases of violation of this ban. A man who had been experiencing business troubles had kidney failure. He and his domestic partner asked a woman, to whom they had lent some money, to donate one of her kidneys. The woman received JPY 30,000 and a small car from the recipient and his partner,

151. https://www.jotnw.or.jp/data/offer.php?year=2020.
152. http://www.asas.or.jp/jst/general/number/.
153. http://www.asas.or.jp/jst/pdf/factbook/factbook2018.pdf.
154. http://jlts.umin.ac.jp/English.html.

and the three were prosecuted. The recipient and his partner were found guilty and sentenced to imprisonment of one year with a suspension of three years (Matsuyama Dist. Ct., Uwajima branch, 26 December 2006), whereas the donor was found guilty in a summary proceeding and was fined JPY 1 million (Uwajima Kansai, 27 October 2006).[155] In another case, a doctor who had kidney failure was sentenced to three-year imprisonment because he had offered money to a donor, who was a member of Japanese Yakuza (Tokyo District Court, 26 January 2012).

§6. Autopsy and Storage/Use of Human Tissue from Cadaver

I. Court Decisions on Dead Bodies and Remains for Interment

111. Before WWII, the Supreme Court decided that dead bodies and parts derived from the bodies of living persons are 'things' and may become the subject of property rights.[156] However, who has the property rights? Before WWII, courts decided that dead bodies or the remains were succeeded by heirs/heiresses. But after the war, courts decided that remains are deemed to constitute 'funeral materials' (graves and family charts) and that they belong to one surviving relative who has been appointed by the deceased, or, if there is no appointment, the one who is to become the master of ceremony according to the custom (Civil Code, Article 897). Recently, a court affirmed claims from a spouse against the brother of the deceased[157] (it should be noted that 'Koshu' (the master of 'house') should have been an elderly man within the 'Ie' (house or family) in the old version of the Japanese Civil Code), and another affirmed claims from a civil partner against the legal spouse and children.[158]

II. Statutes

112. The law concerning human cadavers is provided in two statutes below.

113. The Anatomy and Hold of Cadaver Act was enacted in 1948, soon after Japan surrendered to the Allies. There were two reasons for this enactment. One was that in those days, many died on the road from hunger, so General MacArthur directed the Japanese government to determine the cause of death (corresponding to the coroner/medical examiner's post-mortem). Another was that so many medical schools were instituted during WWII that the need for cadavers for medical education had increased. The Japanese government provided two temporary regulations, respectively, and soon the legislature enacted one statute combining these two.

155. After this case, it also came to light that the urological surgeon involved had performed around thirty 'diseased kidney transplants'. *See* Makoto Mannami et al., *Last Resort for Renal Transplant Recipients, 'Restored Kidneys' from Living Donors/Patients*, 8 Am. J. Transplant. 811–818 (April 2008). Epub 2 Mar. 2008 (presented and written by the surgeon).
156. 27 Minroku 1408 (Sup. Ct., 7 Oct. 1921).
157. 1254 Hanreijihou 70 (Tokyo App. Ct., 8 Oct. 1987).
158. 944 Hanreitaimuzu 238 (Kochi Dist. Ct., 23 Oct. 1996).

This Act provides guidelines for determining the cause of death, dissection in criminal procedure, dissection for administrative purposes (for the confirmation of cause of death without suspicion of criminality, which is done in only five cities in Japan – Tokyo, Yokohama, Nagoya, Osaka and Kobe – and even in these cities there are many problems),[159] dissection in hospitals, and dissection for medical education. Relatives' consent is, generally, needed, but in case of criminal investigation, for administrative purposes and in some specific cases, there is no need to get consent from surviving relatives.

This Act also provides three requirements for keeping cadavers/parts (Table 2):

(1) In university hospitals and some special hospitals, the chief of the hospital may keep cadavers/parts with authorization of surviving relatives (Article 17).
(2) After dissection, doctors may keep parts (not the whole cadaver) without authorization, but they must return them to relatives if the relatives make a claim (Article 18).
(3) Other hospitals may keep cadavers/parts with the authorization of relatives and permission of the governor (Article 19).

Table 2 Types of Preservation of Human Tissue

Object of Preservation		*Purpose*	*Succeeded by*	*Authorization of Relatives*
Article 17	Whole Body and Body Parts	Specimen		Needed
Article 18	ONLY Body Parts	Specimen	Autopsy	Not Mentioned*
Article 19	Whole Body and Body Parts			Needed

* But authorization of surviving relatives for autopsy is generally needed.

114. The Anatomy and Hold of Cadaver Act permits keeping the body if there is authorization from relatives, but in practice, some relatives refuse to give permission in spite of the wish of the deceased. So, a patient group supported the enactment of a new statute that enables dissection for medical education with (only) the deceased's prior consent if there is no refusal from surviving relatives (Anatomical Gift Act).

159. The Act provides as above, but some local authorities have abolished the system so the system now works only in Tokyo, Osaka and Kobe, and it is reported that Osaka will abolish it by the end of the fiscal year 2017. Police records show the rate for autopsy in unnatural deaths is 9%. On the other hand, the Japanese Society of Legal Medicine says that the number of unnatural deaths which were subject to police investigation or death certificate by doctors was 154,579, which was 13.1% of total number of deaths (1,180,280), and that the number of forensic post-mortem examinations was 15,617, which was 1.3% of the total number of deaths.

III. A Case Around Human Tissues

115. There are a few cases concerning human tissues. This may be because the general public does not know of the need for human tissue in medical education and research. One case will show that the above statutes do not fit well with the contemporary situation.

A woman died in a university hospital from systematic sclerosis. After her death, her husband and her son (plaintiff) were asked by the attendant physicians (not by pathologists) to give permission to the hospital for a post-mortem and organ retention. They consented to dissection and retention of the internal organs and brain, and the plaintiff specifically opposed the removal of one finger (it was disputed whether plaintiff opposed the removal of any bone at that time, but it seemed that they did not discuss bones or bone marrow). The plaintiff also insisted on receiving a list of retained organs and a pathological report afterwards.

Pathologists released a summary and later a full pathological report in English to the plaintiff, including the description of 'hypercellular bone marrow', which means that pathologists retained and examined the bone. The plaintiff told pathologists and the head of the hospital that he had meant to authorize only the internal organs and brain, so he wanted whole bones returned. The pathologist explained to him that, in a medical sense, bone marrow was included in internal organs. But the plaintiff was not convinced by this and insisted that all retained organs and tissues should be returned. Accordingly, the defendant pathologist returned the formaldehyde-fixed organs to the plaintiff. But they still kept some paraffin blocks and slides.

At first, the plaintiff claimed on property right. Defendants argued that bone marrow was so important to human body function that removal and retention of the sternum (breastbone) and vertebra (a part of the spine) was done worldwide without surviving relatives' consent (they said this practice was 'common sense of the world'). They also insisted that microscopic specimens should be excluded from 'body parts' in the Anatomy and Hold of Cadaver Act because they could not be substituted by photographs and that they had little nature of remembrance of the deceased by surviving relatives, and that such a claim was abuse of rights because the retention and use of body parts were of great importance to public health and medical education. But the court rejected the defendant's argument and decided for the plaintiff.[160] The reason was that the Act has only administrative effect, so for hospitals to retain organs lawfully, there should have been a contract (gift or bailment) between the surviving relatives and the hospital. Moreover, there must be a relationship of mutual trust between the parties as a basis of such a contract. But in this case, this relationship was destroyed by the defendant's conduct, that is, the plaintiff's opposition to the removal of bone was not properly observed. So, the plaintiff may withdraw his permission. And defendants' pleading on the 'microscopic specimens exception' is without merit because even with the application of work and skill, they are still parts of the corpus.

160. 1738 Hanreijihou 80 (Tokyo Dist. Ct., 24 Nov. 2000).

After that, the plaintiff claimed compensation for emotional distress. But the court rejected his claim.[161] The reason was that while it would be a good practice for doctors to give surviving relatives details of the dissection, including what organs would be removed and that they treat bone and bone marrow as internal organs, at that time, reasonable doctors considered bone marrow as an internal organ which makes blood cells, and reasonable people could imagine that 'pathological dissection' includes removal of internal organs for detecting the cause of death. And it is reasonable not to get explicit authorization from surviving relatives for dissection of an area ordinarily covered with clothes. At that time, 'informed consent'[162] to surviving relatives was not generally in use. So defendants' removal of bone marrow with the authorization on internal organs was not negligent. The court added another reason: Section 17 of the Anatomy Act does not have any provision on claims from surviving relatives, which is provided in section 18. In this case, retention is authorized in section 17, so the defendant hospital does not need to return retained material. Therefore, the court construed the contract as a gift. Although guidelines from the Ministry of Health provide that retained materials should be returned on a claim from surviving relatives without delay, and this would be a good and reasonable practice, breach of this does not give rise to legal responsibility in negligence.

The ruling was appealed by the plaintiff, and the appellate court upheld the judgment of the district court (Tokyo Appellate Court, 30 January 2003); the Supreme Court rejected an appeal.

§7. Medical Research

I. General Description

116. Until recently, the Pharmaceutical Affairs Act and its regulations (corresponding to Good Clinical Practice (GCP)) regulated some parts of medical research as 'Chiken' (clinical trials of new drugs for approval), but other areas were not regulated by statutes. It may be said that medical research was divided into statutory-regulated 'Chiken' and other medical research, although the latter was subject to ethical guidelines. In 2012, post-marketing clinical study on Angiotensin II Receptor Blocker became the target of concern, and two papers were retracted.[163] MHLW established a special committee and an interim report was issued in October 2013. It stresses the need for legal-binding control to clinical study.[164] A bill to regulate clinical research was introduced to the Diet in April 2016 and passed in 2017, and became effective in April 2018. We will see the act in section 118.

161. 1797 Hanreijihou 69 (Tokyo Dist. Ct., 30 Aug. 2002). This judgment was issued by a medical malpractice section of the Tokyo District Court.
162. In Japan, 'informed consent' is (mistakenly) understood as doctors' disclosing information to patients.
163. Eur Heart J. 2013 April; 34(14):1023 and Lancet. 2013 7 September; 382(9895): 843.
164. http://www.mhlw.go.jp/file/05-Shingikai-10801000-Iseikyoku-Soumuka/0000026006.pdf.

II. Statutory 'Chiken'

117. Until the late 1980s, there was no statutory regulation even for Chiken, and foreign pharmaceutical companies and foreign governments criticized the Japanese government's attitude of nonfeasance. In 1989, the Ministry of Health issued regulations titled 'The Standard for Clinical Trial of Medicinal Products' (GCP) by its authority derived from the Pharmaceutical Affairs Act. In 1996, ICH-GCP was issued,[165] and the above standard was amended in 1997. One major amendment was added in 2003 to establish two types of clinical trials; namely, a pharmaceutical company initiated trial (hereinafter referred to as 'company trial') and a physician initiated trial (hereinafter referred to as 'physician trial'). This was because pharmaceutical companies seldom conduct trials for relatively cheap drugs (e.g., aspirin was used as an inhibitor of platelet aggregation outside of approved methods; now it has approval) and for 'orphan' drugs, so more clinical trials were expected by allowing individual doctors to conduct clinical trials. But there are not so many physician trials because of strict requirements in GCP and Good Manufacturing Practice, lack of financial support and vagueness in the nature and position of clinical trials in the introduction of new drugs.

The current GCP provides that those who want to do clinical trials (pharmaceutical companies or physicians) shall make a contract with the hospital (Article 13)[166] and request the principal investigator (Chiken-Sekinin-Ishi, which means the doctor who has the responsibility in the clinical trial) to prepare an informed consent document (Article 9). The administrator of the hospital shall consult a clinical trial committee (Chiken-Shinsa-I'inkai, which corresponds to IRB in the US) and decide whether to conduct the proposed clinical trial (Articles 27–34). After that, the principal investigator, mainly, shall have the responsibility to the subjects he/she chooses (Article 44) to instruct them in the proper use of the drug, and to consult other treating physicians, prepare for adverse events (Article 45), receive informed consent from subjects (Article 50). The principal investigator is also required to make case reports (Article 47) and report side effects to the administrator of the hospital (Article 48). The pharmaceutical company and physician shall monitor and audit the trial (Articles 21–23).

III. Other Medical Research

118. As previously stated, other areas were not regulated by statute, and there was no definition of 'medical research' in statutes or statutory regulations, which

165. www.ich.org/LOB/media/MEDIA482.pdf.

166. In one instance, the Principal Investigator (PI or 'chief principal investigator', Chiken-Toukastu-Ishi) was asked to conduct clinical trials by pharmaceutical companies. It was said that principal investigators were too powerful to keep the trial safe and ethical (e.g., the fee paid by the company was used unclearly, and no one other than doctors had responsibility). So the 'chief principal investigator' system was abolished, and contracts are made between the pharmaceutical company and the hospital. The PI is under the control of both the hospital and the pharmaceutical company. Recently, it has been discussed whether direct contracts between individual investigators and pharmaceutical companies should be allowed; www.mhlw.go.jp/shingi/2007/05/dl/s0518-7a.pdf.

sometimes leads to therapeutic misconception. Doctors often tell patients that there is a 'new therapy' which in fact is an experiment with no established evidence. This custom has been strongly criticized, and some courts permitted claims from the subjects/patients in such cases.

Although medical research other than 'Chiken' is not statutorily regulated (but *see* in paragraph 119), there are sets of ethical guidelines issued by the government.[167] First, genetic research (which is defined as genetic analysis of genes derived from reproductive cells, so it is outside the scope to analyse mutations in somatic cells) was regulated under government guidelines issued by the MHLW, the MEXT and the Ministry of Trade, based on the uniqueness of the human gene. Later, guidelines on epidemiological research were issued by the MHLW and the MEXT, based on the difficulty of obtaining consent in epidemiological research. Finally, all medical research becomes subject to regulation by guidelines for clinical research issued by the MHLW. In the clinical research guidelines, medical research includes both interventional studies and observational studies, and official Q&A states that research is 'systematic investigation designed to develop or contribute to generalizable knowledge', as is the common rule in the US. Based on the Declaration of Helsinki (after the amendment in 2000 at Edinburgh), research using identifiable material or identifiable data is included in clinical research. The latter two sets of guidelines were unified into one single set of guidelines in 2014.

All three sets of guidelines are based on informed consent and IRB approval, although some requirements are different; guidelines for genetic research are the most stringent, guidelines for epidemiological research reflect the nature that it treats many subjects as a mass, and guidelines for clinical research are very general.[168] A recent amendment of guidelines on clinical research requires the research institution to provide no-fault compensation in interventional studies of medicines and medical devices, and researchers to register their research protocol into a public database in an intervention study.[169] Further, the MHLW issued guidelines on conflict of interest, but the guidelines generally leave details to each institution's discretion. Those sets of guidelines become requirements when the institution/researcher receives a government grant, and universities would observe them because they are under the control of the MEXT. But these are just 'ethical' guidelines, so strictly speaking, they have no binding power.

On the other hand, a set of guidelines concerning cloning has statutory authority, and if a researcher does not follow the requirements under the guidelines, it is

---

167. *See* Eiji Maruyama, *Japanese Governmental Guidelines Concerning the Issues*, in *Law and Ethics of Human Tissue Uses* 75 (Matsumura, English, Sato & Utsugi eds 2008), http://jtca.umin.jp/Library/HTW-Proc-081127.pdf; Shimon Tashiro, *Unintended Consequences of 'Soft' Regulations*, 19 Int'l J. Japanese Soc. 4 (2010).

168. The guidelines for clinical research are introduced as 'this set of guidelines expresses the general principles, and details should be considered by researchers and IRBs in individual research protocol'. Further, the requirement of proxy consent is different from guidelines for epidemiological research. In epidemiological research, even a minor (16 years old or more) may give consent, whereas in clinical research, proxy consent of parent(s) is needed (and the minor's assent, if he/she is 16 years old or more).

169. There are three relevant databases in Japan: UMIN www.umin.ac.jp/ctr/index-j.htm, Japan Pharmaceutical Information Center www.clinicaltrials.jp/, and Japan Medical Association www.jmacct.med.or.jp/index.html.

deemed as a violation of the Act on cloning and be culpable; establishment and research use of hES cells is permitted by guidelines issued by the MEXT.[170] Therapeutic cloning is permitted by statute[171] but strictly restricted by guidelines.[172]

IV. Recent Legal Regulations

119. Two statutes regulating research activities should be noted here. One is on regenerative therapy, and another is on commercial clinical research.

Clinical Research of 'regenerative therapy', which uses some kind of stem cells (such as iPS and ES cells) was regulated, and, therefore, permitted by governmental guidelines concerning clinical research using human stem cells. On the other hand, transplantation of stem cells as medical practice was not regulated, so every doctor could provide so-called regenerative medicine. This was highly criticized nationally and internationally, especially after a Korean patient's death in a private clinic funded by a Korean venture company in 2010.

In November 2013, an Act on 'regenerative therapy' was enacted which regulates both clinical research and practice using processed human cells, which requires the provider (hospitals and clinics) submits the plan to MHLW. The provider should receive ethical approval from one of the ethics committees which are certified by the MHLW.

Furthermore, as stated above, the pharmaceutical company's commitment to clinical research was highly criticized, and the MHLW decided to enact a new statute to regulate the clinical research funded by commercial companies. The act, that was passed in 2017, and became effective in April 2018, defines clinical research as 'research to clarify the efficacy or safety of pharmaceuticals by the use of such pharmaceuticals in humans' and regulates 'specific clinical research', which is defined as (i) a research which receives research fund from pharmaceutical companies, (ii) research using non-approved drug or device or using drug or device outside the approved requirement (dosage and indication).[173]

§8. Quarantine and Medical Care to Combat Infectious Diseases

120. Japan has been experiencing, and also suffering from, the spread of COVID-19 caused by SARS-CoV-2. The government declared the state of emergency in Tokyo four times in eighteen months; from 7 April to 25 May 2020, from 8 January to 21 March 2021, from 25 April to 20 July 2021, and from 12 July to 31 August 2021. During the period we had five surges and hospital bed shortage caused big problems especially in January and April 2021.

---

170. *See* Cynthia B. Kohen, *Renewing the Stuff of Life* 154–155 (2007). The guidelines are available at www.lifescience.mext.go.jp/bioethics/hito_es.html; the old version is available in English www.mext.go.jp/a_menu/shinkou/seimei/2001/es/020101.pdf.
171. www.cas.go.jp/jp/seisaku/hourei/data/htc.pdf.
172. www.mext.go.jp/a_menu/shinkou/seimei/2001/hai3/31_shishin_e.pdf.
173. English translation is available at https://www.mhlw.go.jp/file/06-Seisakujouhou-10800000-Iseikyoku/0000213334.pdf.

The Japanese government handled this issue by (amending and) enforcing the Quarantine Act, Infectious Diseases Act (Act on the Prevention of Infectious Diseases and Medical Care for Patients with Infectious Diseases (the Infectious Diseases Control Law),[174] and the Act on Special Measures against Novel Influenza, etc., which was enacted in the surge of novel influenza in 2012 and amended in 2020 to handle COVID-19.

The Quarantine Act provides a prohibition of entering Japan from foreign countries without authorization, and in case of specific diseases including COVID-19, without medical tests. But it has been criticized that quarantine stations at even large international airports lack proper testing devices (most quarantine stations have no equipment for PCR testing, so they use only antigen tests instead of PCR tests), and that to use PCR tests, saliva samples have to be transported to laboratories outside the airports. The act also provides isolation in positive cases, but quarantine stations generally 'request' isolation in specific hotels for four to eleven days.

The Infectious Diseases Act provides tests and medical examinations followed by involuntary hospitalization and request for self-isolation. As stated above, hospital bed shortage made it impossible for patients who needed hospital care to be hospitalized, so self-isolation at home and requested stay in hotels were common; on 3 August 2021, the government issued a policy that prefectures may limit hospitalization only to patients with severe conditions and that mild and moderate ill patients will not be able to be hospitalized but stay home, which is criticized even by the ruling party. Furthermore, death cases at home were not counted officially by MHLW (some data were collected and provided by the National Police Agency[175]).

174. https://www.mhlw.go.jp/stf/seisakunitsuite/bunya/kenkou_iryou/kenkou/kekkaku-kansenshou/taiyakuhyou/index.html.

175. From 1 Jan. 2020 to 30 Jul. 2021, 536 death have been detected by prefectural police; 489 at home and 47 outside home. https://cdp-japan.jp/files/download/c8XS/CNrx/BoNO/kiad/c8XSCNrxBoNOkiadnfqBb4JV.pdf, https://cdp-japan.jp/files/download/AlrA/QC7c/nU7j/G7Eb/AlrAQC7cnU7jG7EbYBz1jw1k.pdf.

Part III. The Physician and the Healthcare System

Chapter 1. Relationship with Other Healthcare Providers

§1. PHARMACISTS

121. The Pharmacists Act provides the filling of prescriptions as an exclusive practice of pharmacists. But, as described in General Introduction Chapter 2 §1, making drugs has long been understood as a doctor's role, so the Act permits exceptions that allow doctors to make drugs on their own when the patient or caregiver asks for drugs from the doctor, or when there are other medical reasons (Article 19; *see also* Doctors Act, Article 22). Until recently, the patient's wish was presumed, and doctors made and dispensed drugs even if the patient said nothing about a prescription. But now, it has become customary for doctors to hand a prescription to patients, who then receive the drug from an outside pharmacy.

§2. MIDWIVES

122. Midwifery is a traditional profession (midwives were called 'Samba') in the same way as Kan-pou doctors. But for quite some time it has been considered one of the medical professions. After WWII, the statutes regulating Samba and Kangoshi (nurse) became one statute, and Samba was renamed 'Josanshi', which means those who assist birth. The Act on Nurses and Midwives provides that those who are not midwives may not provide midwifery and hygienic direction to pregnant women, women after birth, or newborns, other than provided by doctors (Article 30).[176] The Act also provides that nurses and midwives may not use medical devices, provide medicine, or provide other procedures which have a hygienic risk if not under the direction of a doctor or dentist (Article 37; exceptions are in an emergency and in a midwife's own practice). It also provides that midwives must let the patient see a medical doctor if they find something wrong (such as dystocia) with the pregnant woman, a woman after birth or a newborn (Article 38).

176. It is not clear whether a doctor may use a nurse to examine the dilation of the cervix. Recently, police investigated a hospital suspected of breaching the Act on Nurses and Midwives, but this case was not prosecuted and the court's opinion was not issued. The MHLW seems to think that examination by a nurse is illegal, but doctors oppose this stance; www.jaog.or.jp/news/images/01Feb2007.pdf.

123. The statute demands that a midwifery clinic make a contract with (at least one) physician for emergency cases (Article 19, Medical Care Act), and the regulations under the statute provide that the physician should be an obstetrician/gynaecologist (Article 15-2, Regulations). It is said that many midwives have trouble finding a consulting physician because of the doctor shortage.

§3. Nurses

124. Doctors may delegate some of their work to nurses. The Act on Nurses and Midwives provides that nurses are those who practice patient care and assist in medical care (Article 5). The latter part is construed as a basis of such delegation. Nurses should get an attending doctor's direction when using medical devices and providing medicine (Article 37, described above). The delegated practice may be delegated to other healthcare technicians, as described below. Increasing nurses' practice is under discussion in MHLW committee, and the Act will be amended in a few years; it is said that it will be provided in the amendment that nurses who receive training may provide some kind of medical practice with doctor's general order (protocol).

As described above, a doctor must supervise and give direction to nurses, and if he/she fails, the doctor may be liable in both civil and criminal law.

§4. Other Healthcare Technicians

125. Other healthcare technicians may practice part of the above-delegated practice of nursing. Emergency medical technicians (Kyukyu-kyumei-Shi) may provide life-saving treatments such as vasopressin and insertion of a tracheal tube. In hospitals, medical laboratory technicians may draw blood and do examinations of the body (which are considered medical procedures), as well as laboratory examinations (which are not considered medical procedures and so anyone may do them). Physical therapists, occupational therapists and speech therapists may also provide rehabilitations, which are considered medical procedures.

Chapter 2. Relationship with Healthcare Institutions

126. As described above, doctors working in a hospital are employees of the hospital, and hospitals and private practice clinics are independent. Traditionally, doctors also belong to 'Ikyoku' (a medical school department such as first internal medicine; usually, medical schools have three internal medicine departments and two surgery departments). The professor of the department is the head of the Ikyoku and has absolute power in hiring and firing doctors, transferring doctors to another (usually rural) hospital and so on, and young doctors move among hospitals in rural areas according to the professor's direction. But now, large hospitals in urban areas independently employ young doctors. That leads to a problem: young doctors who do not belong to Ikyoku are increasing, and doctors are shorthanded in rural areas. As discussed above, some public hospitals in rural areas have closed because of doctor shortages and deficits. This became the subject of public debate, and some candidates for city mayors have pledged the continuance of public hospitals as an election promise.

Chapter 3. Others: Minister's Direction

127. During WWII, the Minister of Health and Welfare had the authority to direct doctors, but such authority was abolished after the war. This authority was restored in the Doctors Act after a case of syphilis contracted through transfusion became known.[177] Article 24-2 provides that the MHLW may direct doctors on medical or health issues if there is a special need to prevent big problems in public health, but the Minister must consult the Committee of Medical Affairs before issuing the direction. At one time, a 'Standard concerning transfusion which doctors or dentists should follow' was issued, but was abolished (or rather was amended and substituted with new and more detailed guidelines). There are many sets of guidelines, but they are not issued through the above process. So, whether they are legally binding is not clear except in socialized health insurance, where government guidelines are prerequisites for reimbursement.

177. *See* Part 1 Ch. 3 §3 II C.

Selected Bibliography

Bai, K. *Iji Hougaku Eno Ayumi.* Tokyo: Yuhikaku, 1970.

Iida, H. & I. Yamaguchi. *Keiji Iryou Kago I II and III.* Hanrei Taimuzu, 2001, 2007 and 2013.

Kai, K. *Bridge Book, Ijihou.* Tokyo: Seibundo, 2008.

Kai, K. et al. *Ijihou Hanrei Hyakusen.* 2nd edn. Tokyo: Yuhikaku, 2014.

Mark A. Colby. *The Japan Healthcare Debate: Diverse Perspectives.* Kent, UK: University of Hawaii Press, 2004.

Ministry of Health, Labour and Welfare. *Kousei Roudou Hakusho* (White Paper, published annually) www.mhlw.go.jp/english/wp/index.html.

Noda, Y. *Ijihou.* Tokyo: Seirinshoin, 1987.

Robert B. Leflar. 'Informed Consent and Patients Rights in Japan'. *Houston Law Review* 33 (1996): 1.

Shigeto, Y. *Ijihou Kougi* Tokyo: Nihon Hyouronsha, 2016.

Tejima, Y. *Ijihou Nyumon.* 3rd edn. Tokyo: Yuhikaku, 2011.

Utsugi, S. & Y. Tsukamoto. *Gendai Iryou No Supekutoru.* Tokyo: Shogakusha, 2000.

Some judgments of the Supreme Court may be downloaded at http://www.courts.go.jp/app/hanrei_en/search.

Selected Bibliography

Index

The numbers here refer to paragraph numbers.

Index

www.ingramcontent.com/pod-product-compliance
Lightning Source LLC
LaVergne TN
LVHW021113300926
849160LV00009B/724
* 9 7 8 9 4 0 3 5 4 1 1 2 9 *